World Religions and Beliefs

Founders OF Faith

World Religions and Beliefs

Founders
OF Faith

By Joan A. Price

MORGAN REYNOLDS
P U B L I S H I N G

Greensboro, North Carolina

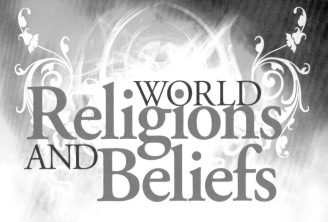

WORLD Religions AND Beliefs

Founders of Faiths

Mystics and Psychics

The Birth of Christianity

The Birth of Islam

World Religions and Beliefs: Founders of Faith

Library of Congress Cataloging-in-Publication Data

Price, Joan A.
Founders of faiths / by Joan Price.
   p. cm. -- (World religions and beliefs)
Includes bibliographical references.
ISBN 978-1-59935-147-6
1. Religious biography--Juvenile literature. 2. Religions--Juvenile
literature. I. Title.
BL72.P72 2011
200.92'2--dc22
                                        2010038441

Printed in the United States of America
First Edition

To my dear study-group friends:
Bernadette, Claudia, Diane, Gina, Irene, Ruth

Contents

Introduction

he true foundations for most of the world's major religions—the exact manner in which each came to be—are forever lost in the mists of time.

No one can say for sure, for instance, who the first Hindu was; or in which Mesopotamian city the first Jews lived; or the circumstances under which the Buddha became enlightened; or precisely how Jesus viewed his mission in life.

To fill in these and other gaps in the formative stages of the leading faiths, myths have emerged over the course of many centuries. Today, unfortunately, the term *myth* is often used to denote something false or invented. The tale of the ancient Greek hero Perseus slaying Medusa, a monster whose gaze turned people to stone, is a common example.

However, in their original, purer form, myths were, and remain, traditional stories about cherished gods and the founders of faiths. They answer vital questions about humanity's past and the relationship between God and humans. Examples include God commanding Abraham to kill his son; demons threatening the Buddha while he searched for enlightenment; and an angel rolling away the stone blocking the entrance to Jesus's tomb. Even though no tangible evidence now exists for these and many other traditional religious stories, people continue to believe them as a matter of faith. And that, after all, is what religion is all about.

Of these age-old tales, among the most fundamental and familiar are those that tell how the religions themselves came

to be. In many cases these faiths were the visions or handiwork of a single, extraordinary person. And usually that individual was said to be inspired or somehow guided by God. As H. W. F. Saggs, a historian of ancient times, put it, "Most major religions of the world—Christianity, Hinduism, Islam, [Judaism] and Buddhism—and a host of minor ones, have received their imprint from the teaching of a great religious reformer, who, according to believers, brought a direct divine revelation [connection with and/or instructions from God]." For the Jews there is Abraham, for the Persians Zoroaster, and for the Muslims Muhammad.

One important exception to the scenario of a divinely guided human founder is Hinduism. No traditional Hindu tale of a single, larger-than-life human organizer has survived. This may be because Hinduism is considerably older than the other major faiths and that all memories of its beginnings have been lost. As Saggs points out, "The mainstream of Hinduism has continued without imposed change since prehistoric times (although it has undergone gradual evolutionary modification)."

It is unknown, therefore, exactly when the Hindu faith, originally called the Vedic faith, began to emerge. The best guess of modern scholars is that it happened sometime in the fourth millennium (the 3000s) BCE. It was in this period that India's first advanced civilization, which was not uncovered and recognized until the twentieth century, was forming. Archaeologists dubbed that early people and their culture "Harappan," after one of their chief cities, Harappa, in western India (now the nation of Pakistan). The Harappans, it turned out, had the distinction of creating the world's first pre-planned towns and cities. According to one noted scholar:

Harappa, along with the other Indus Valley cities, had a level of architectural planning that was unparalleled in the ancient world.

The city was laid out in a grid-like pattern with the orientation of streets and buildings according to the cardinal directions [north, south, east, and west]. The city [also] had many drinking water wells, and a highly sophisticated system of waste removal.

Initially, historians thought that an aggressive outside people—the Aryans—invaded and overthrew the Harappans and introduced a new culture—the Vedic. However, the scholarly consensus has become that no such invasion took place. Instead, the Vedic culture grew directly out of the Harappan one. That means that the most sacred writings of Vedic culture, and the early Hindu religion, the *Vedas*, may have begun to take shape in Harappan times, or maybe even earlier.

The *Vedas* consist primarily of verses, some of which are sacred hymns, others prayers, and still others religious instructions. These Hindu scriptures are based on belief in a universal or supreme spirit called Brahman. He supposedly gave rise to, or in some accounts assumed the form of, three other spirits, or deities. These were Brahma, the creator god; Shiva, god of destruction; and Vishnu, the preserver god.

Vishnu himself took a number of forms or guises, called incarnations or avatars, in which he came to Earth to perform various services or heroic deeds. Among them were Kurma, Rama, and Krishna. Krishna appears particularly prominently in the *Bhagavad-Gita.* It is part of a larger Hindu literary work, the *Mahabharata*, which appeared a few centuries after the *Vedas* did. The *Mahabharata* describes a huge war in which the Pandavas, the sons of a legendary emperor named Pandu, defeated their wicked cousins, the Kauravas, with Krishna's help.

As a great hero, therefore, Krishna is a major figure in Hindu mythology and is tremendously popular among all Hindus. They see him as the god who could transform sinners into saints, ignorant people into sages, and even animals into devotees. Also, he came to Earth to protect the forces of good, to destroy the forces of evil, and to establish justice. In addition, he is viewed by one Hindu denomination, Krishnaism, as the supreme being. It is fitting, therefore, in looking back on the origins of Hinduism, to examine Krishna's story more closely. True, he did not establish the Hindu faith. And indeed, as a legendary character his very existence cannot be proven. Yet his exciting, inspiring story personifies and in many ways captures the colorful, larger-than-life spirit of the early Hindu faith and its majestic, often moving sacred writings.

Chapter

1

Krishna

The story of Krishna, often called Lord Krishna by the faithful, begins about 5,000 years ago in the ancient Indian city of Mathura. At the time it was ruled by Kamsa, a tyrant who had forcefully taken the throne from his father, King Ugrasena, and imprisoned him. The usurper had a sister, Devaki, and when she was old enough, he arranged her marriage to one of his nobles, Vasudeva.

Not long after the marriage took place, a sage told Kamsa that the eighth son of Devaki and Vasudeva would destroy him and overthrow his kingdom. To prevent this prophecy from coming true, the king threw the newly married couple into prison and killed the first six children that Devaki bore. She eventually conceived a seventh time. But unbeknownst to anyone, the

Almaty · Urumqi · GOBI · A

S · I A

KYRGYZSTAN · Yumen · Yinchuan

TIKISTAN · CHINA

Hotan · Chengdu

Kashmir

Islamabad

NEPAL · Lhasa

New Delhi · BHUTAN

Jabalpur · BANGLADESH

INDIA · MYANMAR (BURMA)

Kolkata

Hyderabad · Yango · THAILAND

BAY OF · Bangkok

BENGAL

Bangalore · Chennai

SRI LANKA · Kuala

Sri Jayawardenepura

unborn child was Balarama, Vishnu's divine elder brother. The baby was miraculously taken from Devaki's womb and placed in the womb of Vasudeva's second wife. (It was common in ancient India for some men to have multiple wives.)

While Devaki and Vasudeva were still in prison, Devaki conceived an eighth time. The god Vishnu appeared to them with the news that their new child, a son, would be his own avatar. Legend relates that he was born at midnight with very dark blue skin and a little curl of hair on his chest. They named him Krishna (meaning dark-skinned).

Immediately following the birth, the parents heard a disembodied voice. It gave Vasudeva instructions to take their newborn to the chief of the cow-herders, Nanda, and his wife Yasoda in the village of Gokula. The voice ordered Vasudeva to leave Krishna with the couple and bring back the girl-child who had just been born to them.

To save the divinely begotten child, Krishna, the gods made the prison guards go to sleep and unlocked all the iron gates to allow Vasudeva outside the jail. Carrying out his instructions, Vasudeva smuggled Krishna across the Yamuna River to the village of Gokula. There he secretly exchanged his son, Krishna, for their baby girl and carried her back to his wife Devaki.

The sage had distinctly told King Kamsa that the eighth child would be a boy. So when he saw the girl-child, he hesitated. At that moment, the child revealed her true identity to the king. She was the fierce, demon-fighting goddess Durga. The goddess informed Kamsa that the newborn boy was safe and that he lived within a radius of ten miles of the palace.

Realizing he had been tricked, the angry king sent out demons that could take any shape and fly through the air. He ordered them to kill all newborn male children within a radius of ten miles.

However, these evil creatures were unable to slay Krishna, who, though only a baby, easily outwitted and destroyed them.

The Young Prankster

As that infant Krishna grew into a child, he often got into mischief. In one case, he smeared himself with mud and made mud pies to eat. When Yasoda scolded him, he said, "Mother, I didn't eat any mud." He urged her to "look into my mouth yourself." When Yasoda did so, she saw there the whole universe, including the Earth, oceans, mountains, and valleys, along with all the planets and stars. Because this was something only the gods were supposed to see, they quietly drew over her a veil of forgetfulness.

According to the Hindu writings, the young Krishna played other miraculous pranks as well. One day, for example, he paid a fruit-seller with a handful of rice instead of money. When the woman arrived home, she found that each grain of rice had turned into a jewel. Another time, Krishna broke some vessels containing milk and curds and ate the butter. To punish his behavior, Yasoda fastened a rope around his body and tied him to a large bowl. However, Krishna dragged the bowl away until it got caught between two trees and uprooted them. From this feat he earned the nickname Damodara, meaning "rope belly." Krishna also frequently stole butter and cream and shared them with his friends and with the monkeys and birds. Not wanting him to grow up to be a thief, his foster mother tried to tie his hands together so he could not steal. But the rope soon grew too short to tie.

When he was five years old, Krishna's foster family moved from the village of Gokula to the forests of Vrindaban. Accompanied by his divine elder brother Balarama, Krishna helped care for their father's herds. In the forests he spent days with the herder girls, called gopis, and herder boys. They played tag and leapfrog and raced over the fields to the music of Krishna's flute. His usual mischievous self, he also played tricks on them from time to time. On one occasion, when the gopis were bathing in a river, Krishna snatched their clothes and climbed up a tree. He remained there until the girls came to him naked to recover their attire.

Every year the cow-herders of Vrindaban offered sacrifices to the nature deities. They asked for rain and good crops and healthy herds. Intent on putting an end to nature worship, Krishna went to Nanda and other villagers. He urged them to worship the one true God, Brahman and his trinity, made up of Brahma, Vishnu, and Shiva. He taught them to understand that good or bad harvests came from their own actions and not from pleasing nature deities. He explained that health and wealth were the effects of their thoughts and actions in past and present lives. Brahman, the supreme God, Krishna said, was greater than all the nature deities put together. Nature deities were merely forces of Brahman. Worshiping the nature deities was like worshiping the rays of the sun rather than the sun itself.

As the story goes, Krishna's teaching so angered the nature deities that they sent down pouring rain. The river overflowed and torrents of water uprooted trees and washed them away. Never had the village experienced such a flood. To help the villagers, Krishna told them to bring their cattle and possessions to the mountain. Then with a single finger he lifted the mountain and allowed everyone to take shelter beneath it. For seven days and seven nights, the people huddled safely under the mountain. At last the nature deities, realizing they were no match for the incarnation of Vishnu, repented and offered worship to Krishna.

Death of a Tyrant

More time went by and Krishna approached manhood. He was so handsome that the gopis were all enamored of him, and he married at least seven of them. But his first and favorite wife was Radha. At this period of his life, according to the legends, he had blue skin and dark flowing hair and carried his flute almost everywhere. In fact, one of his favorite pastimes was to play music, to which he, Radha, and the cow-herders danced.

But Krishna's happy life in the fields was rudely interrupted when King Kamsa, who still feared and hated the young man-god, sent more demons to destroy him. Like the earlier attempts on his life, this one failed. So Kamsa next decided to hold a festival in Mathura, during which he hoped he would be able to kill Krishna. When the celebration was ready to begin, the king sent a messenger to invite everyone in the kingdom, including Vasudeva, Devaki, Nanda, Yasoda, Krishna, Balarama, and all the cow-herders.

They all accepted the invitation and journeyed to Mathura. Among the festivities was a wrestling exhibition in an arena. There, Kamsa sent in his strongest wrestlers to fight Krishna. The first wrestler, who had large, muscular arms, came down heavily on Krishna, but the latter leapt aside, seized his opponent, lifted him above his head, and tossed him onto the ground. Seeing this, the next wrestler sprang forward, followed by a third and a fourth. But hardly breaking a sweat, Krishna lifted each of them above his head and threw them out of the arena.

Then Krishna jumped from the arena right into the royal box, where the king was sitting. Beside the king was a sacred bow, a weapon made by the gods. It was well known to all in the kingdom that no one could take away the king's crown and depose him unless they had first bent and broken this fabulous weapon. And, no living person had ever managed to achieve that feat.

Before anyone could stop him, Krishna grabbed the bow, strung it, and then pulled the string back so far that the weapon broke in two. The enraged king ordered his soldiers to capture Krishna. But using the broken bow, he easily drove them back. Then King Kamsa drew his sword, intending to slay Krishna. But the young man grasped the ruler by the hair, after which the royal crown fell off onto the ground and Kamsa, unable to withstand Krisha's great strength, died.

An artist's impression of Krishna (top) killing King Kamsa, and Balarama, Krishna's older brother, killing one of Kamsa's wrestlers

With the evil tyrant out of the way, Krishna restored the rightful king, Kamsa's father Ugrasena, to the throne. Krishna and his brother Balarama stayed awhile in Mathura and studied the *Vedas* and other sacred writings. Krishna also studied military science under a wise teacher. Having gained much knowledge, he came to give advice to various local Indian rulers, who eagerly followed his suggestions. They erected splendid cities and brought Indian culture to new heights of power and efficiency.

Krishna and Arjuna

Krishna was happy to see all this progress. But he did notice one potential problem. Namely, the military strength of the Indian kingdoms grew so large that it endangered the prosperity and the lives of everyone. He wanted the leaders to lessen this danger by reducing the size of their armies. But it was not his way to interfere too much in worldly affairs, so he decided to sit back and allow events to transpire in their own way.

Krishna did not realize that a clash of armies even bigger than he envisioned lay in the immediate future. The events leading up to that fateful conflict began with a major public contest. Krishna's cousin, the princess Draupadi, daughter of the king of the Panchala kingdom, had grown old enough to become a bride. And brave knights from all over India journeyed to her father's kingdom to compete for her hand. The winner would have to shoot an arrow into a bull's-eye from a bow almost impossible to pull. Among the candidates were some of India's most celebrated heroes. Among them, five knightly and courageous brothers, princes of the kingdom of Kuru, greatly impressed Krishna. One of them, Arjuna, strung this bow and managed to shoot his arrow right into the center of the target. No other contestant hit the bull's-eye, so prince Arjuna won the royal bride.

Arjuna and his four brothers were the good Pandava princes, the sons of King Pandu, who were destined to rule India.

Krishna and Arjuna in a scene from the *Mahabharata*, one of two major Sanskrit epics of ancient India. The eighteenth century ink-on-paper painting is on display at the Smithsonian Freer Gallery of Art and the Arthur M. Sackler Gallery.

Their wicked cousins, the Kauravas, had exiled the five princes thirteen years earlier and during their absence the kingdom had grown corrupt. After long wanderings and hardships, the brothers had formed an army. And with Arjuna as its military general, they hoped to regain the kingdom that was rightfully theirs.

The events of the ensuing war, along with Krishna's

spiritual teachings and advice to Arjuna about the meaning of life, are the substance of the *Bhagavad Gita.* The epic opens on the plains of Kurukshetra, where the two armies faced each other. Arjuna stood proudly in his chariot and right beside him was Lord Krishna. Arjuna asked Krishna to drive the chariot into the space between the two armies so that he could survey the enemy's strength. When Arjuna saw that many of his relatives, friends, and childhood comrades were in the enemy ranks, he suddenly gave in to grief and despair. Throwing down his weapons, he refused to fight.

But Lord Krishna reminded Arjuna that he was a member of the warrior caste (social class) and that it was his duty to fight to bring good out of a bad situation. If necessary, warriors must protect the good by military force, Krishna told Arjuna. And the duty of the warrior caste is to rule righteously and see that society receives the justice it deserves. He explained that different types of people made up society. By nature humans fell into one of four social castes—the sages, the administrators, the producers, and the laborers. The administrator caste included warriors, and Arjuna was a warrior. So it was his duty to fight. A warrior, Krishna said, must not throw down his weapons, because a wise warrior sees all men as God sees them—as immortal souls. War can kill people's bodies, but the immortal soul can never die. "Just as you throw out used clothes and put on other clothes, new ones," Krishna continued, the soul "discards its used bodies and puts on others that are new."

Krishna explained that the life of the body depends on the soul. The soul needs the body it inhabits only as much as the body needs the clothes it wears. When the body wears out its usefulness, the soul leaves and the body dies. When the soul is ready for birth again, it creates a new body. (This process of the soul being born into a new body in life after life, which Hindus believe in, is known as reincarnation. Each life on earth is an experience the soul needs to progress toward human perfection. All human souls share the same goal—to become perfect in the knowledge and love of God.)

Krishna taught Arjuna that reincarnation embraces the law of karma. Essentially, he said, karma ensures that what goes around comes around. Karma holds that for every action there is an opposite and equal reaction. So each deed, good or bad, that a person performs affects the world in some way and comes back to affect the person in some way. Therefore, whatever happens now, in the present life, can be and often is the result of past actions in a former life.

Hearing this tremendous outpouring of wisdom, Arjuna asked Krishna if he was a god. Krishna answered, "I am the soul, Arjuna, seated in the heart of all beings; I am the beginning and the life span of beings, and their end as well." Krishna added, "I support the whole universe with a single fragment of myself." He informed Arjuna that from time to time he descended to Earth to reestablish spiritual purity.

War and Departure

Arjuna then asked how a person can realize God in their lives. Krishna told him that a person can do so through the discipline of yoga. Yoga means to yoke or unite the powers of the body, mind, and soul to God, who lies hidden in one's deepest being. Krishna then explained the various methods of yoga.

Finally, Arjuna asked if he could see Krishna, not just as his human-looking charioteer, but as the divine being he really was. As they stood there on the field of battle, Krishna decided to reveal his true form to his friend Arjuna. Stunned, the young prince abruptly found himself standing before something both unimaginable and magnificent—a being having the sun and moon for eyes, a body as huge as the entire universe, and a soul of pure goodness capable of residing in the heart of every human.

At that instant, the thoroughly impressed Arjuna felt himself move from ignorance to knowledge. He saw his duty as a warrior clearly and all hesitation drained from him. Springing to his feet, he sounded the war cry of the Pandavas and flung himself into battle.

Eighteen days later, the Pandava princes and Krishna stood uninjured and victorious. But all around them stretched countless piles of dead bodies. Queen Gandhari, mother of the defeated Kauravas, wept for her slain sons. Overcome with anger, she blamed Krishna for the bloodshed. If he had wanted to, she said, he could have prevented the massacre. When Krishna offered no answer, she cursed him to die alone in the wilderness in thirty-six years. Krishna said, "I gladly accept your curse."

For the next thirty-six years, Krishna acted as advisor to the king of Mathura. Their country was rich and the people happy. Bountiful harvests kept them in good health and good spirits. But in the midst of prosperity, certain lords of the king's court angered visiting divine sages and the sages cast a curse on Mathura. It called for the people to go mad and exterminate one another.

The king took the matter to Krishna, but the latter saw the world as a drama. As a spectator would watch a play acted out, Krishna watched world events take place. He watched cities prosper and crumble, wars and interludes of peace, and broken treaties and kept treaties. Through all of this, he kept telling himself that the law of karma would even things out in the end.

As time went on, the people of Mathura could not avert the calamity. Many people died and day after day strong winds blew. The streets swarmed with rats, which ate all the grain stored for the people; cranes started hooting like owls; goats brayed like donkeys; sons killed fathers; fathers slew sons; and in the sky planets collided with constellations.

Krishna watched it all calmly, holding an iron thunderbolt in his hands. And eventually he sensed that the time for his own death was nearing. At the end of the thirty-sixth year, Gandhari's curse calling for Krishna's death became a realty. He prayed to Brahman, and then sent for Arjuna and asked him to govern

Krishna's life is depicted in nine separate panels in this painting from the early to mid-1800s by an unknown Indian artist. The panels are not in chronological order: Beginning from the top left and moving horizontally, the themes are Radha and Krishna; Krishna stealing the clothes of the bathing cowgirls; Krishna tied to the mortar in the twin Arjuna tree incident; Krishna destroying the horse-demon Keshi; Krishna slaying the calf-demon Dheruka; Krishna quelling a forest fire; infant Krishna killing the ogress Putana; the submission of Brahma; and a prince or poet paying obeisance to the enthroned Krishna.

Mathura. Krishna promised the citizens of Mathura that Arjuna would be their protector and would see to all their needs. Then he left the palace for the solitary forest.

When he reached the depth of the wilderness, Krishna laid down on the ground and silently meditated. Soon a hunter mistook him for a crouching deer and shot an arrow that struck Krishna in the heel. When the hunter saw what he had done, he fell to the ground, apologized, and touched Krishna's feet. The wounded god blessed and comforted him. Then Krishna ascended into a state of bliss, filling the universe with his splendor. He was 125 years old, and according to legend he was never again seen in the world of humans.

Chapter

2

Abraham

The founding father, so to speak, of Judaism, the religion of the Jews, as well as of the Jews themselves, was an aged man named Abraham. Abraham, who appears in the Bible's first book, Genesis, is unique among the founders of the world's major faiths. He not only established the ideals and some of the rituals that initiated the rise of the Hebrew (later called Jewish) people. He was also a key figure in the foundation of two other leading world religions. Both Christianity and Islam recognize Abraham as the first true monotheist (believer in a single god). Moreover, Muslims see him as their earliest prophet and mention him in their daily prayers. And he appears frequently in the writings and rituals of Christianity, which evolved directly out of Judaism.

Opposite Page: *The Sacrifice of Isaac*, a 1634 painting by Rembrandt van Rijn depicting an angel preventing Abraham from killing his son, Isaac. The painting is on display at the Hermitage Museum collection in St. Petersburg, Russia.

As is true of all the founders of ancient religions, Abraham remains largely a mysterious figure. The few surviving ancient documents that mention him, including the Bible, say almost nothing about his life before he was an old man. And they are at best sketchy about his later years. As a result, he emerges as a semi-mythical figure, in a sense an archetype (original version or model), in this case the archetype of the Jew.

Indeed, as the ancestor of all later Jews, Abraham displayed certain personality traits that later came to be associated with that people. As rabbi and scholar Ken Spiro puts it:

I call Abraham 'the proto-Jew.' He personifies everything that could be characterized as the 'Jewish personality.' His strengths, mission, drive, and idealism are reflected in all the generations of the Jewish people that come after him. Abraham was certainly one of the great truth-seekers of all time. He was also famous for his kindness and hospitality. But the attribute that probably stands out more than any other and truly [captures] the essence of what Abraham, and therefore the Jewish people, is all about, is drive. To stand alone for thousands of years against the entire world; to dedicate oneself, heart and soul, to the ultimate cause of perfecting the world requires tremendous strength of character. This drive is an outstanding feature of Abraham's personality and we see its manifestation in every generation of the Jewish people. From Abraham onward, we see this idealism—an uncompromising drive to 'change the world'—in the collective Jewish personality.

The Wrong Ur?

The world that Abraham changed through his travels and actions was already quite ancient when he was born. It consisted almost entirely of the Near East (today called the Middle East), stretching from what are now Afghanistan and Iran in the east, to the Arabian peninsula in the south, to Palestine (along the Mediterranean coast) in the west. His original homeland, lying in the very heart of the Near East, was the series of then fertile plains known for millennia as Mesopotamia. The term Mesopotamia derives from Greek words meaning "the land between the rivers." It is a reference to the Tigris and Euphrates rivers, which flow across the Mesopotamian plains and empty into the Persian Gulf.

For a long time, modern scholars thought that Abraham was born near the shores of that waterway, in the city of Ur. Ur probably started as a small village in the fifth millennium (the 4000s) BCE. In the fourth millennium (the 3000s) BCE, a resourceful people now known as the Sumerians transformed Ur into one of the world's first true cities. It eventually had numerous streets, houses, and shops, along with temples, palaces, tall defensive walls, and tens of thousands of residents. In the late third millennium BCE, Sumerian Ur reached its height of power. For a brief period it was the center of an empire that historians call the Third Dynasty of Ur, or Ur-III for short, which controlled large portions of Mesopotamia. Soon that empire declined. And by the early second millennium BCE the city had become a largely quiet center of religious ceremonies and learning.

Ur must have been an imposing, inspiring sight in its prime, in the 2000s and early 1000s BCE. However, it is quite possible that Abraham never beheld that sight. The reason that experts long thought it was his hometown is that the Bible seemed to say so. Genesis identifies Ur of the Chaldeans as the city in which Abraham was born and raised. The assumption was that Ur of the Chaldeans was Sumerian Ur, situated near the Persian Gulf.

However, Genesis was composed many centuries after Abraham's death. And scholars now think its writer (or writers?) was mistaken.

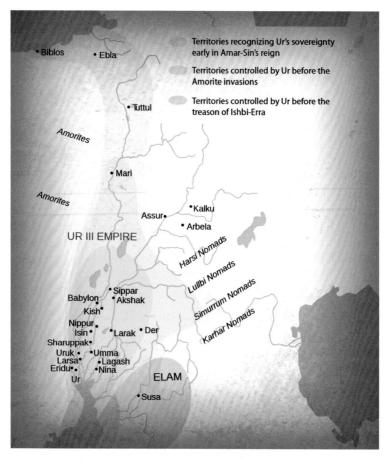

A map of the Ur-III Empire in Mesopotamia in the twenty-second century BCE

Sumerian Ur was located far to the southeast of the other Mesopotamian towns initially associated with Abraham and the earliest Hebrews. Among these towns were Harran (or Haran) and Ebla. Archaeologists discovered that a town called Ura existed in northwestern Mesopotamia near Harran and Ebla. Ura was a busy trading center. This is noteworthy because several ancient sources suggest that Abraham was a merchant of some kind. In addition, the descriptions in Genesis of Abraham's travels only make sense if his native town was in northwestern Mesopotamia. According to the renowned twentieth-century scholar Cyrus H. Gordon:

It is probable that Ura (which would come into Hebrew as Ur, without the final vowel) [was] Abraham's birthplace. [The Ur mentioned in Genesis] can hardly be [Sumerian] Ur in the south. Genesis 11:31 tells us that Terah [Abraham's father] moved from Ur [to] Harran en route to Canaan [Palestine]. Any route from [Sumerian] Ur [to] Canaan would not go so far north or east as Harran. [Therefore] the Ur [mentioned] in Genesis has to be north or east (probably northeast) of Harran for Terah's itinerary [list of destinations] to make sense.

Thus, Genesis seems to say that the homeland of the ancestors of the Jewish people was not in Palestine, but in northwestern Mesopotamia. Archaeologists are able to verify this in large part because of the names of several towns discovered in the region. These are almost identical to the names of Abraham's brother, grandfather, and great-grandfather, among others. Also, an inscription found in Ebla mentions that one of its ancient kings was named Ebrum. And Ebrum is the name from which the word *Hebrew* derived. Finally, the people of Ebla spoke what modern language experts have identified as an early version of Hebrew.

A Family on the Move

It appears that Abraham's family lived in the area of Ebla and Ura for a very long time before the more famous events of his life occurred. Genesis says that his father, Terah, was descended from Noah. According to the Bible, the latter had been instructed by

God to build a large boat (the ark) in order to survive an enormous flood that almost destroyed humanity. Terah had three sons while living in Ura—Abraham, Nahor, and Harran. After Harran had a son of his own—Lot—Harran died.

Then Terah gathered together his other sons and their families and moved to the nearby town of Harran (for which his dead son had been named). By that time, Abraham was married to a woman named Sarah. But they had no children because she was unable to conceive. A passage in Genesis reads:

Terah took Abraham, his son, and Lot, the son of Harran, his grandson, and Sarah, his daughter-in-law, his son Abraham's wife, and they went forth together from Ur of the Chaldeans [and] when they came to Harran, they settled there.

Terah died in Harran at the age of 205, according to Genesis. Apparently this was the point where the pivotal events in Abraham's life began to take place. When he was seventy-five, again according to Genesis, God came to him and said, "Go from your country and your kindred and your father's house to the land I will show you. And I will make of you a great nation, and I will bless you and make your name great." The "great nation" referred to here would later turn out to be the Hebrew/Jewish people and their God-given homeland in Canaan/Palestine.

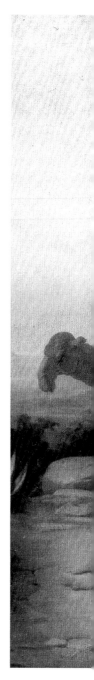

Abraham's Journey from Ur to Canaan, the 1850 painting by Jozsef Molnar,
is on display at the Hungarian National Gallery in Budapest, Hungary.

Doing as God commanded, Abraham took Sarah and his nephew Lot, along with their servants and flocks of sheep, and journeyed to Canaan. There, they settled for a while on a piece of land pointed out by God. Abraham built an altar there so that he could make offerings of thanks to the deity who had befriended him.

Not long after the family's move to Canaan, a famine struck the region. Because it was difficult to find enough food for his family and servants, Abraham migrated toward the southwest and into Egypt. The amount of time he and the family spent there is unknown. More certain is that Genesis says they eventually returned to Canaan, which suggests that the famine there had ended.

Abraham the Military Leader

For an undetermined period of time, Abraham and his family members prospered in the land that God had granted them. Eventually, after some minor disagreements, Abraham and Lot decided to go their separate ways. Lot moved with his family to the region near the Dead Sea containing the towns of Sodom and Gomorrah. (Later, a famous biblical story relates, Lot escaped mere minutes before God destroyed those two cities because their citizens were sinners.) After the separation with Lot, Abraham resettled in Hebron, an area located a few miles south of the small town of Salem, which would later grow into the Jewish capital city of Jerusalem.

More time passed. Then suddenly and unexpectedly some foreign invaders appeared from the east. It is difficult to tell who they were exactly from the scant evidence available in Genesis and other surviving ancient documents. But evidently they consisted of an alliance of four or more Mesopotamian cities that were seeking to exploit whatever riches they could find in Palestine. The intruders forced the local Canaanite towns to give them tribute (money or valuables paid to acknowledge their submission).

For twelve years the Canaanite towns, including those in which Abraham, Sarah, and Lot lived, paid the tribute. But finally they felt they had had enough. So they rebelled and refused to pay any more. That triggered a second invasion by the intruders from the east, who defeated the Canaanites and took several captives. Among these prisoners was Lot. If the section of Genesis dealing with this crisis is correct, by this time Abraham had charge of a small army of followers. Perhaps they were local townsmen who looked to him as their military leader because he was older and more experienced. In any case, Genesis says:

When Abraham heard that his kinsman had been taken captive, he led forth his trained men . . . three hundred and eighteen of them, and went in pursuit, [and] he divided his forces against them [the invaders] by night, [and] routed [defeated] them and pursued them to Hobah, north of Damascus [in southern Syria]. Then he brought back [his] kinsman Lot.

Abraham returned to Canaan in triumph. The king of Salem blessed him for his courage. And the ruler of Sodom offered him a rich reward. Genesis says that Abraham refused this generous prize so that the man who offered it could not later claim that Abraham was beholden to him. This was only one example of Abraham's renowned honest and upright character.

Historians have tried to identify these invaders who entered Palestine from the east, along with the time frame of the military campaigns involved. Some say the events in question were likely fabricated by the authors of Genesis, who wrote that tract many centuries later. However, other scholars, including the widely respected Kenneth Kitchen (of the University of Liverpool), suggest that the invasions of Canaan mentioned in Genesis may be based in fact. Various aggressive Mesopotamian city-states did make raids into Palestine in the early second millennium BCE, Kitchen points out. Among the states that might have been involved were Elam, Eshnunna, Mari, and Babylon. Scholars are unable to determine if a Canaanite named Abraham fought the raiders. But these studies at least provide a possible chronology for estimating when Abraham lived (assuming he was a real person).

The Conception of Ishmael

It was impressive enough that a man who was in his late eighties could lead men in battle. But Abraham now topped that by fathering a child. Sarah apparently felt bad that she was still unable to conceive and bear her husband a son. So she made a deal with her Egyptian maid. This young woman, named Hagar, agreed to become a second wife to Abraham so that he would have a chance to father a son.

When Hagar became pregnant, however, Sarah grew jealous and changed her mind. She chased Hagar away and the young woman fled into the desert wilderness. There, according to Genesis, an angel sent by God found her and told her not to fear. She should return to the house of Abraham and Sarah, the angel said, adding: "I will so greatly multiply your descendants that they cannot be numbered for [their] multitude." Then the angel told her, "Behold, you are with child and shall bear a son. You shall call his name Ishmael."

The "numberless multitude" to which Ishmael was destined to give rise turned out to be the Arab people. It is doubtful that anyone could have known this at the time. So many scholars think the angel and his prophecy were added after the fact, perhaps to

The Dismissal of Hagar, a 1612 oil painting on wood by Pieter Lastman, on display at the Hamburger Kunsthalle in Hamburg, Germany

strengthen the idea that the Jews and Arabs both came from a common ancestor. That ancestor, of course, was Abraham.

The Covenant with God

One might naturally ask how Abraham could have given rise to the Jews if his only son, Ishmael, went on to father the Arabs. The answer is that Abraham had a second son, Isaac. And Isaac's mother was Sarah, whom everyone had thought could not have any children.

The manner in which this unexpected event occurred was bound up in the larger matter of a major and historic deal struck between Abraham and God. When Abraham was ninety-nine, Genesis says, God appeared to him and said that he wanted to make a covenant, or agreement, with him. Genesis claims that the Lord told the aged Canaanite:

I will make my covenant between me and you and will multiply you [make you sire children] exceedingly. [I] have made you the father of a multitude of nations. I will make you exceedingly fruitful. And I will make nations of you, and kings shall come forth from you. And I will establish my covenant between me and you and your descendants after you throughout their generations. [And] I will give to you, and to your descendants after you, the land of . . . Canaan, for an everlasting possession. And I will be their God.

If this incident actually took place, it stands to reason that Abraham would have wondered why God had chosen him for this important honor. Certainly biblical scholars and other experts have long speculated about why God needed Abraham. The most popular consensus is that God needed a human he could trust after many others had let him down. For example, Adam had sinned in the Garden of Eden; several generations later widespread bad behavior by men and women had driven the Lord to bring on the great flood; and later still, humans had angered the deity by trying to erect the Tower of Babel, in an attempt to reach heaven. "After so many failed experiments," acclaimed author Bruce Feiler writes,

God needs a new kind of human. He needs someone faithful, who won't disobey him and who will appreciate the blessings that he has to offer. Above all, God needs someone who needs him and who will rise to his lofty standards. He needs Abraham.

Sealing the Covenant

For whatever reason God chose Abraham, according to the writers of Genesis, a crucial deal had been made between the two. This formerly obscure Mesopotamian, who had moved to Palestine, had become the father of a new group of people yet to come. Moreover, that people had been purposely chosen to be the Lord's special followers thereafter. "This is my covenant," the deity told Abraham, "which you shall keep, between me and you and your descendents after you."

To seal the deal, God told Abraham that there was to be a unique requirement, one that all Jews would be expected to fulfill from now on. Namely, the males of that people would have to be circumcised. (Circumcision consists of the removal of the foreskin of the penis, usually when the person is a baby, though it can be done at any age.) God told his new prophet:

You shall be circumcised in the flesh of your foreskins, and it shall be a sign of the covenant between me and you. He that is eight days old among you shall be circumcised. Every male throughout your generations, whether born in your house or bought [as a slave] shall be circumcised. . . . Any uncircumcised male who is not circumcised in the flesh of his foreskin shall be cut off from his people. He has broken my covenant.

Having dealt with the circumcision issue, God now addressed the matter of how Abraham would manage to father this new race—the Jews. Sarah would be blessed and have a child, a new son, God told him. She would therefore become the mother of the new chosen people.

Could a man who was almost a hundred years old father a child? And what about Sarah? She was now ninety. How could she be expected to bear a baby? God answered that the child would come to be born because he, God, would make it happen. "Sarah, your wife, shall bear you a son," the Lord insisted, "and you shall call his name Isaac. I will establish my covenant with him as an everlasting covenant for his descendants after him."

As for Ishmael, God said, he would not be slighted. He would also become the father of a great nation. Although the Lord did not specifically say so, it was understood that that nation would be separate from the Jews. (As already pointed out, tradition says it was the Arabs.)

A Troubling Order

Once more, time passed. And Genesis says that Sarah bore the son that God had prophesied. She and Abraham did as the Lord had commanded and named the boy Isaac. When Isaac was eight days old, again following God's orders, Abraham circumcised the child. Later, when Isaac was weaned (no longer needed to be breast-fed), his parents had a big feast to celebrate.

At some point when Isaac was a bit older, and Abraham was over a hundred, God visited his elderly prophet still again. This time, what the deity had to say sorely troubled Abraham. God instructed him to take the boy, go into the mountains, and sacrifice him. According to Genesis, God said:

‘Abraham!’ And he [Abraham] said ‘Here am I.’ He [God] said, ‘Take your son [Isaac] whom you love, and go to the land of Moriah, and offer him there as a burnt offering upon one of the mountains of which I shall tell you.’

The reason that Abraham was troubled had to do with the enormity of what God had ordered. In those days the religious ritual of sacrifice was extremely common among all peoples and faiths across the Middle East. It consisted first of selecting an animal, usually a sheep, goat, or cow (but sometimes other creatures). The animal was led to an outdoor altar. There, the person performing the sacrifice took a sharp knife and slit the animal's throat, killing it. Next, the person butchered the sacrifice, putting aside certain organs or other parts. These were burned and the smoke rose up into the sky. The general belief was that this smoke nourished and pleased the god (or gods) in whose name (or names) the ceremony was performed. (Often, the rest of the victim's body was cooked and eaten by the worshipers.) It was clear, therefore, that God wanted Abraham to kill Isaac and burn parts of his body to satisfy the deity.

On the Altar of God

Abraham did not flinch at God's order. He went to bed that night. And the next morning he arose, gathered together Isaac, two servants, a donkey, and some wood for the burnt offering. The group traveled for three days. Isaac apparently knew there was going to be a sacrifice. Several times along the way he asked his father where the animal was that they would be offering to God. Each time Abraham answered that the Lord would provide the animal when the time came.

When they reached the mountain God had chosen, Abraham told his servants to wait beside the trail. The father said he and Isaac would go the rest of the way together. Carrying the wood for the offering, Abraham led his son up the slope until they reached the spot that God had selected. There, the aging man built a makeshift altar. Then he bound Isaac with ropes, laid him on the altar, and pulled out a knife, intending to cut the boy's throat.

But at the last moment, Abraham heard a voice from high above and hesitated. The voice said: "Do not lay your hand on the lad or do anything to him." Abraham lowered the knife and untied Isaac. Then he saw movement out of the corner of his eye and noticed a ram caught in a nearby bush. Abraham now realized that he had been correct when he had said that God would provide an animal for the offering. So he went ahead and sacrificed the ram.

Then, Abraham named the spot where he had erected the altar "The Lord Will Provide." Today, Jews preserve a rocky knoll in Israel, which long-standing tradition claims is the place where the ancient prophet nearly sacrificed his son. Whether or not it is actually the spot, no one knows for sure. More certain is that many famous men later stood on the knoll, among them Israel's King Solomon, Jesus, and Muhammad. Today countless worshipers and tourists visit what Feiler describes as "a magnet of monotheism, an etched, worn mask of limestone . . . hidden under a golden dome, and made more powerful by the incandescence [glow] that seems to surround it at every hour."

A Test of Faith

A question often asked by those who visit the rock is why God demanded that Abraham slay his son and at the last minute intervened to stop him. The most common answer is that it was a test of faith. In other words, God was testing his prophet. According to this view, the Lord wanted to make sure that Abraham, unlike Adam and others before, would obey him without question.

An even more important question for many people has been posed numerous times over the centuries: Why was Abraham so willing to obey God and kill Isaac? The prospective answers to this question have also been numerous. Some people have suggested that Abraham knew all along that God would not allow the boy to die. So the man simply went through the motions, waiting for God to intervene. Another theory is that Abraham thought he had to kill Isaac because the boy belonged to God. And if Abraham refused to go through with the sacrifice, God would slay everyone in the family as a punishment. A third possibility is that Abraham did not know that God

The seventeenth-century painting *Sacrifice of Isaac by Abraham* by Peter Paul Rubens, on display at the Louvre Museum in Paris, France

would intervene, but hoped he would. This was because he trusted God to do the right thing.

A fourth possible answer has been proposed less frequently but is no less believable than the others. This one points out that, at least as told in Genesis, God never specifically told Abraham to kill the boy. Rather, the deity simply ordered him to take him to the mountain and make an offering of him. Once the child was bound and lying on the altar, the test was complete. In that case, the act of raising the knife to slay Isaac was instigated by Abraham. And if so, it was Abraham's way of *testing God,* not the other way around. Maybe Abraham wanted to make sure that God would keep his promise to create a new race of people from Isaac's descendants. That promise obviously could not be kept if the boy was killed on an altar.

A Will to Survive

Whoever it was who was being tested that day, Isaac lived on to give rise to the Jewish people. As for Abraham, he lived many more years. He moved from Hebron to Beersheba, in what is now southern Israel. There, Sarah died at the age of 127. And after grieving her, Abraham, now close to 140, married again. His new wife, Keturah, was said to have had six sons by him.

After living what no one can deny was a long and eventful life, Abraham died at the age of 175, according to the book of Genesis. His first two sons, Ishmael and Isaac, buried him in the Cave of the Patriarchs, in Hebron. That series of underground caverns, where Isaac, too, was supposedly later interred, still exists. It is one of the holiest sites for Jews, Christians, and Muslims alike. As such, it is another of the many reminders that Abraham was the patriarch, or father-figure, for three great world religions.

The Jews hold Abraham especially fondly in their hearts, however. They contend that without him and the covenant he formed with God, they would not exist. Max Dimont, the twentieth-century scholar of Judaism and author of *Jews, God and History*, put it this way:

After four thousand years, the idea of a covenant between the Jews and [God] is still alive and mentioned daily in prayers in synagogues throughout the world. Though many aspects of Jews and Judaism have been changed or modified during their subsequent four-thousand-year history, this idea of a covenant with God has remained constant. This in turn gave rise to a will to survive as Jews, which has been the driving force in Judaism. Without it, there can be no Judaism and no Jews.

Chapter

3

The Buddha

Like Hinduism and Judaism, Buddhism is one of the world's oldest religions. Over the course of many centuries Buddhism spread throughout Asia and gained some followers in the Western world as well. But its beginnings were in ancient India, and it arose from the spiritual awakening of a single extraordinary man.

In the sixth century BCE India was in a state of religious upheaval and political instability. The widespread use of iron tools and weapons had revolutionized farming and warfare in the preceding few centuries. The plains of northern India, nourished by the Ganges River and its many tributaries, were growing

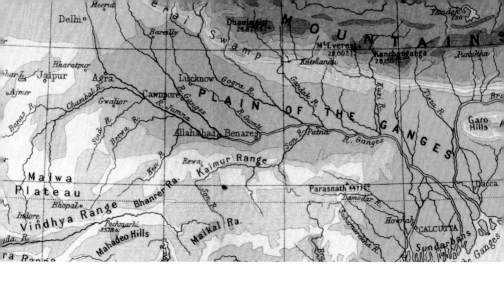

into lush farmlands with numerous cultivated crops. As expanding population claimed more and more land, the region's thick forests were disappearing. City states and villages ruled by tribal leaders were giving way to centralized kingdoms and empires. The man who came to be called Buddha, or "the" Buddha, himself lived to see the land of his clan, the Sakyas, overrun by the kingdom of Kosala. Later, Kosala itself fell under the power of the formidable Magadha Empire.

There was also growing religious turmoil in India at the time. It was caused in part by the Hindu social order called the caste system. This system included four *varnas,* or social groups, of people: the Brahmins, who were spiritual leaders and priests; the Kshatriyas, administrators and warriors; the Vaishyas, artisans and businessmen; and the Sudras, menial laborers who served the upper classes.

For hundreds of years the powerful Brahmin priests asserted their rights to religious and social authority. During this time when the masses were passively relying on the priests to tell them what to do, some intellectuals began to question the priestly religion. As a result, a number of schools of philosophy grew up that taught new ways of thinking and challenged the values of the priestly caste.

The Birth of a Prince

Into this world of social, political, and religious turmoil was born Siddhartha Gautama (or Gotama), who was destined to become the Buddha. His exact birth date, like most of the events of his life, remains unknown. But tradition places that birth in 563 BCE in Lumbini, an ancient kingdom at the foot of the Himalayas in northeast India (now Nepal). His full name was Siddhartha Gautama of the Sakyas. Siddhartha was his given name, Gautama was his surname, and Sakya was the name of the clan to which his family belonged. His father, Shuddhodhana,

was an Indian king of the Sakya clan and a member of the Hindu warrior caste.

A number of omens (supposedly divine signs of important impending events) were later said to herald Siddhartha's birth. In one, his mother, Queen Maya, dreamed that a white elephant appeared in her bedchamber. According to one of the surviving popular legends about the Buddha's early years:

> In his [the elephant's] trunk, which was like a silver rope, he held a white lotus. Then, trumpeting, he entered the golden mansion, made a right-wise circle three times around [Maya's] bed, smote [struck] her right side, and appeared to enter her womb.

The next morning the queen related her dream to the king and together they summoned the wisest sages in the kingdom to interpret the dream. These dream-readers predicted that the queen would bear a gifted son who in adolescence would face two possible futures. If he stayed always inside the palace, he would become a king. But if he began living outside the royal residence he would become a poor monk or hermit. Not surprisingly, Shuddhodhana wanted his son to grow up to be a king, like himself. So he became determined that once the child was born, he must be kept inside the palace at all times, and if necessary forever.

When the boy came into the world, the king and queen named him Siddhartha. Seven days after the birth, Queen Maya died in her sleep and her sister, Prajapati Gotami, took on the task of caring for young Siddhartha. He grew into an amazingly gifted child. And like other boys of well-to-do families of his day, he received the best education possible. Because he belonged to warrior caste, from an early age he was also trained in military affairs. The young prince did well in everything he undertook. And when he was not learning how to become a warrior he spent his days studying languages, the Hindu scriptures, mathematics, science, and music. He mastered arts such as riding and archery, and vigorously played with his companions.

A Sheltered Youth

The king tried his best to divert the young prince's attention away from life and society beyond the palace, hoping to prevent the young man from gaining a desire to leave. Shuddhodhana knew full well that outside the royal residence existed sickness, pain, death, and other unhappy realities of life. And he wanted his son to be spared knowledge of such things.

As a result, at age twelve Siddhartha had yet to experience pain. His first lesson in that unwanted aspect of life occurred one day in the spring when his cousin Devadatta shot a wild swan flying north to its nesting grounds. The bird fell to the ground wounded and the prince picked it up, soothed it, and removed the arrow from the wound. The boy could clearly see that the bird was suffering.

Devadatta ran over and demanded the swan, but Siddhartha refused. They argued and finally decided to take the problem to their elders. As it turned out, some of the elders thought the swan belonged to the prince, while others thought the swan belonged to the cousin. After much discussion, one elder commented that a life should belong to the one who tries to save it and not the one who tries to destroy it. The other elders agreed and they gave the wounded swan to the prince.

One day Siddhartha accompanied his father to the rich fertile fields that one day would be his. While the king spoke with an overseer, the prince walked through the gardens. He saw a lizard eat an ant, and a snake swallow the lizard. Biting flies and mosquitoes raised welts on the oxen plowing the field. Also, at the edge of a pond he saw frogs snatching insects with a flick of the tongue. The prince sat down beneath a rose-apple tree to meditate on what were to him new, unusual, and sad things.

Soon, according to legendary stories about the Buddha, two of the king's attendants came upon Siddhartha as he sat in meditation under the tree. But the young man was unaware of his surroundings and his face had a look of absolute calm. The attendants noticed that the shadows of all the other trees in the garden had moved with the passage of the sun, but the shadow of the rose-apple tree that Siddhartha sat beneath had remained where it was to shade the prince.

News of his son's deep meditation disturbed the king. Siddhartha had all the strength and beauty of a prince, but he showed little interest in courtly life. To keep his son from seeing the sometimes unpleasant realities of the outside world, King Shuddhodhana beautified the palace grounds and gave the prince three large, splendid cottages. A Buddhist text credits the prince with saying:

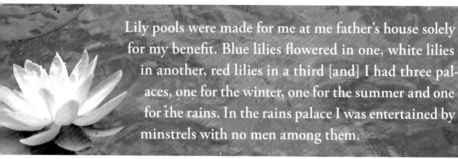

Lily pools were made for me at me father's house solely for my benefit. Blue lilies flowered in one, white lilies in another, red lilies in a third [and] I had three palaces, one for the winter, one for the summer and one for the rains. In the rains palace I was entertained by minstrels with no men among them.

When Siddhartha was sixteen, the king's advisors suggested that a wife would help to keep the prince's attention on courtly life. So the search for a bride began. After considering all the eligible girls in the kingdom, the advisors selected Yashodhara, who was also sixteen and the daughter of a Shakya nobleman. But according to the custom of the time, Yashodhara had to be won in a contest by the man who could bend a bow, wield a sword, and ride a horse better than all others. As it turned out, Siddhartha shot his arrows at a greater distance into the bull's-eye than any of his opponents. Then he strung and shot a bow that no other man had the strength to draw or string. With his sword, Siddhartha cut straight through two trees, and he tamed a fiery black stallion that none of the other contestants could ride. Undefeated in all the competition's events, Siddhartha won Yasodhara's hand in marriage.

Learning of Life's Sorrows

For several years the prince and his wife lived the life of royal householders in luxury and ease. Because of the prophecies that attended Siddhartha's birth—that he would become either a kingly ruler or an impoverished holy man—King Shuddhodhana made every effort to keep his son secluded from the sorrows of the world, to hide from him the unpleasant truths of old age, sickness, and death. Thus Siddhartha, along with his wife, dwelled unaware of these things. In spite of the enjoyable diversions of the royal court, however, Siddhartha remained detached and listless. It was as if deep down inside he suspected that there might be more to life than what he already knew.

All that began to change on a day when the young prince went riding outside the palace. The king sent runners along with him to clear the roads of anyone who was old, sick, or dying, so that Siddhartha would not see them. But on this day things did not go as planned. The runners did not perform their job well enough, and the prince saw a man he described as "bent as a roof gable, decrepit, leaning on a staff, tottering as he walked, afflicted and long past his prime." For the first time, Siddhartha had learned of the existence of old age.

Though the king doubled his guard, the next day Siddhartha met a man thin and weak, raging with fever and racked with disease. On a third journey, he saw a corpse lying cold and stiff on a litter with mourners following behind, weeping and beating their breasts. Siddhartha rode to the outskirts of the city for a place to meditate. He needed to think long and hard about the sorrows of old age, sickness, and death, which, he had suddenly learned, all physical beings must experience.

While he was still outside the city, Siddhartha encountered a monk with a shaven head, wearing a yellow robe and carrying a begging bowl. The monk's face was calm and filled with joy. When Siddhartha questioned him, the holy man said he had left his home in search of a kind of happiness that lay beyond old age, sickness, and death. Having renounced all material things, he carried the bowl for bits of food from the charitable. That was all he asked of the world.

Struck by the man's serenity, Siddhartha abruptly realized that the path of the holy monk was the very path he must also follow. "I will [cut] off my hair," the prince said, "and don the yellow robe, and go forth from the house into the homeless state." That, he reasoned, would better allow him to search for enlightenment—knowledge of how to find contentment in a world full of sorrows and suffering.

The Search for Enlightenment

Soon afterward, during a night in his twenty-ninth year, Siddhartha made the fateful break from his life of luxury. He entered the room where his wife and newborn son, Rahula, slept and bade them both a silent goodbye. Then he hurried to the stable where his charioteer had his horse saddled. When they reached the edge of the forest, Siddhartha dismounted and the chariot eer returned with the horse to the palace to break the news to the king. With his sword, Siddhartha cut off the knot of hair that signified his princely station in life. Legend relates that a beggar appeared wearing a garment of coarse yellow cloth. Siddhartha exchanged clothes with him and then hastened into the forest in search of enlightenment.

A giant statue representing the Buddha, called *Tian Tan Buddha* (the Big Buddha), at Po Lin Monastery on Lantau Island, Hong Kong

Day and night Siddhartha meditated searching for life's ultimate truths. He ceased meditation only when hunger drove him into a village for enough food to stay alive. For weeks meditation filled him with joy. Then temptations plagued him, including the desire for his wife and a longing to see his father and son. As a result, he began to doubt his ability to find the truth or to save the world from suffering. Day and night he wrestled with these doubts while lost in the wilderness. At one point, the legendary accounts say, he said, "Rough is the road [and] the struggle [is] desperate."

At last Siddhartha overcame the voices of doubt that had been tempting him to abandon his quest. He now sought out Alara Kalama and Uddaka Ramaputta, two famous Hindu wise men known throughout India. His intention was to pick their minds to seek the wisdom they had amassed during their travels and meditations. From them Siddhartha learned a great deal about Hindu philosophy. And he soon became quite cultured and wise in his own right. To his regret, however, his knowledge still fell short of complete enlightenment. So he continued his search.

One day in the forest Siddhartha met five monks who also yearned to find enlightenment, in their case by practicing severe bodily disciplines, including denying themselves many of lives pleasures. Among other things, they ate very little and abstained from sex. They invited Siddhartha to share their life of sober austerity and he agreed. With them, he practiced severe bodily discipline, hoping to find liberation from the sorrows of the world. A Buddhist text credits him with this description of his plight:

My body reached a state of extreme emaciation [thinness]. My limbs became like the jointed segments of vine stems [and] my backside became like a camel's hoof. The projections [bones] on my spine stood forth like corded beads [and] my ribs jutted out as gaunt as the crazy rafters of an old roofless barn.

It was said that Siddhartha reached a point where he could touch his backbone through his stomach. His dark eyes nearly disappeared in deep hollows and he became so ill that when he stood up, he fainted. During his illness, he came to the conclusion that this strict regimen of fasting and self-mortification was not the path to enlightenment for him. The starvation and its effects only dulled his mind and senses. And he felt that there must be another, better way.

To renew his health, Siddhartha started eating and drinking normally again. "As soon as I ate the solid food, the boiled

rice, and bread," he
later recalled, "the five
[monks] were disgusted and
left me, thinking: 'The monk
[Siddhartha] Gautama has become self-
indulgent, [and] has given up the struggle
and reverted to luxury.'"

Enlightenment at Last

Six years had passed since Siddhartha had left his home
and begun following a monk's life. Although his mind was
calm and peaceful, he had yet to reach the ultimate realization he
sought—a spiritual awakening. For days he wandered alone, still
diligently trying to attain that goal.

Eventually, near the Indian city of Gaya, Siddhartha found a spot
under a tree that ever after has been called the Bodhi-tree. (In the
language spoken in ancient India, the term *bodhi* means "enlightenment.") Hoping that he would finally be able to attain his goal,
he folded his legs beneath him and took a solemn vow: "Come what
may—let my body rot, let my bones be reduced to ashes—[but] I
will not get up from here until I have found the way beyond
decay and death."

While sitting beneath the tree, Siddhartha struggled with various temptations. Evil demons approached and tempted him to abandon his virtuous quest because, they claimed, his family needed him. One tempter, Mara, who took the form of a god, informed him that his cousin had imprisoned his father and taken control of his wife. But Siddhartha ignored the demons and sat unmoved. When more demons attacked him with their deadly swords, he touched the ground with the fingers of his right-hand. And this contact with the earth produced a loud, thunderous noise that frightened the demons away.

After the hideous creatures had fled, what seemed to Siddhartha to be an ocean of truth poured into his mind and heart. Suddenly entering a state of pure bliss, he felt that he could behold the past, present, and future simultaneously. The mysterious secrets of birth and death and how people passed from one life into another opened to him. He also seemed to acquire the ability to comprehend the eternal laws of the universe. The ecstasy of this incredible experience kept him rooted to the spot for seven entire days. On the eighth day he tried to rise, but another wave of delight broke over him. For a total of forty-nine days he was lost in the joy of learning great truths. The clear light of spiritual knowledge was at last his. Prince Siddhartha had become the Buddha—the enlightened one.

During his great acquisition of enlightenment—ultimate knowledge of the world and life—the Buddha came to realize that everything in the world changes and decays. Nothing is constant, neither animals nor people, nor their personalities or feelings, nor even ideas. He saw that all life is an evolving process, like an ever-moving stream.

His First Disciples

After meditating on his momentous discovery, the Buddha journeyed to Banaras, where he found the five monks who had worked so hard to discipline themselves in their own search for enlightenment.

Legend relates that these men at first looked at their former companion with contempt. They remembered him as the prince who refused to practice strict enough discipline. So they refused to rise from their seats when he approached, nor would they even give him a simple greeting.

As the Buddha drew closer, however, they could see his face shining with a sort of miraculous glow, which they realized could only have come from acquiring vast knowledge. Suddenly their standoffish mood changed and they greeted him amiably and sat at his feet. To these monks the Buddha proceeded to deliver his first teachings. He taught them first of the Middle Way, where one neither mistreats the body nor follows sensuous pleasure. He spoke to them of the Wheel of the Law, in which, he explained, all life is interconnected.

The Buddha also told the monks about what Buddhists came to call the Four Noble Truths. The first is that human life is full of suffering. The second truth is that selfish desire and endless craving for what is pleasurable is the main cause of suffering. Third, there is a way to avoid suffering. And fourth, the way to escape from suffering is to let go of traditional, selfish desires and begin to follow the Eightfold Path.

That path is a list of "right," or beneficial, goals and achievements. They include: right understanding, right thought, right speech, right action, right livelihood, right effort, right mindfulness, and right concentration. All people need to think and speak truthfully; set ethical, constructive goals; behave honestly and justly; make a living in a manner that does not harm others; and meditate to make sure he or she is on the right track. By following these rules, the Buddha said, people can find Nirvana, a state of peace, selflessness, harmony, and happiness.

When he had completed his initial sermon, the five monks realized that he had attained enlightenment. They avidly became his first disciples, or followers. And not long afterward, they established the order of Buddhist monks known as the Sangha.

Preaching to the People

News of the Buddha's enlightenment spread swiftly. Wherever he went people crowded about him, eager to hear about what he had learned about life's mysteries. As he traveled, he gathered a following of many who wanted to become monks in the hope of gaining enlightenment like he had. The only requirement he insisted on was a sincere desire to follow the Middle Way. It meant leaving one's family, just as he had done, and leading a simple but disciplined life of celibacy and strict morality. While he lectured groups of interested people, some of his closest followers journeyed into neighboring villages to carry his message of compassion and self-discipline.

During his travels, Buddha decided to share what he had learned with the family he had left seven years before. His father the king, his wife Yasodhara, his young son Rahula, and many others from his clan, along with people from surrounding areas, gathered at the river. There he explained about suffering and its causes, as well as the workings of the stars, the sun and moon, and the oceans. He also asked them to shun evil and follow the good life.

Hearing these words of wisdom, several of his family members entered the path of peace and meditation. His stepmother, Prajapati Gotami, started an order for nuns, and his son Rahula decided to become a monk. After bidding his family goodbye, the Buddha and his disciples traveled to more Indian villages and cities to teach. And his fame drew people from near and far.

During the rainy season, when the monsoon clouds gathered over the land and rain poured down, the Buddha and his followers visited monasteries. There they engaged in discussions and debate.

And frequently they won over those who opposed their views with the clarity, conviction, and beauty of those ideas. As a result, many in the monasteries got rid of Hindu caste distinctions and joined the growing ranks of the Sangha order.

But though a number of the Buddha's teachings were new, he had not abandoned all Hindu principles. He retained and taught the law of karma, for instance, in which words and deeds from a person's life can affect him in his next life. To this traditional view, he added the notion that practicing the tenets of the Eightfold path can free a person from some karmic burdens.

The Buddha's Final Days

The Buddha successfully won over numerous people to his views. However, his lifestyle and teachings were not without controversy and opposition. Some of those who clung to older beliefs tried to discredit him by creating scandals. One such person was his cousin Devadatta, who wanted the Buddha to leave the leadership of the Sangha to him. According to tradition, when the Buddha refused to do what Devadatta wanted, the latter tried to kill the enlightened one by throwing him in front of a mad elephant. But the force of Buddha's boundless compassion supposedly made the beast turn away.

Another ancient story claims that Yasodhara's father insulted the Buddha in public. It appears that the older man was angry that the Buddha had deserted his daughter and become a monk years before. Again, the Buddha called on the forces of love and compassion, in this case to change his father-in-law's heart.

The Buddha was said to have encountered and appeased other opponents in the forty-five years in which he traveled from place to place teaching the meaning of justice, love and righteousness.

He told people that they should look within themselves for enlightenment. "Be a lamp unto yourselves," he said. "Rely on yourselves and on nothing else."

At age eighty, perhaps around the year 483 BCE, the Buddha died. The exact cause is unknown. But according to tradition it was dysentery (a bacterial infection of the intestines). Even on his deathbed, the story goes, he thought and spoke of others rather than himself. Tradition also says that he stretched out in a lion posture, lying on his right side with one foot on the other. This pose can still be seen today in huge statues carved of him in later ages.

The dying Buddha sent a follower into the city of Kusinara to tell the people that he would likely pass away that night. Anyone who wished to do so could come to see him for the last time. A number of men, women, and children gathered to pay their last respects and to receive the Buddha's blessing. It was to them that he allegedly spoke his last words. Decay is inherent, or built into, all things, he said. He added: "Work out your own salvation with diligence." Then his eyes closed for the last time.

For Justice and Human Rights

Following his passing, the Buddha's teachings steadily grew into a religion that in time divided into two main branches: Theravada Buddhism and Mahayana Buddhism. Like Jesus, the Buddha left no writings behind. Unlike the case of Christianity, however, there is no one book of sacred scripture for all Buddhists. Buddha's teachings were memorized and recited for several centuries before they were written down. The scriptures that guide followers of Theravada Buddhism are known as the *Pali Canon* and were written around the first century BCE. That work is divided into three sections, together called the *Tripitaka,* meaning "three baskets." Together the three baskets could fill a medium-sized bookcase. Among the

Mahayana scriptures are the *Prajnaparamita Sutras,* the *Lotus Sutra,* the *Diamond Sutra,* and the *Dhammapada.*

Today, because the Buddha emphasized nonviolence, many Buddhists are social activists who protest oppression, famine, animal cruelty, war, and environmental pollution. One widely recognized representative of such social activism is the Dalai Lama, a native of Tibet and great Buddhist spiritual leader. Living in exile in northern India, where he fled two years after Communist China occupied Tibet in 1957, he lectures around the world on justice and human rights. In the spirit of Buddhism, the Dalai Lama motivates others to relieve human and animal suffering in the world. His speeches are not only beneficial to all people, but also a fitting tribute to the great thinker and teacher who founded his faith.

Pages from the original *Pali Canon,* circa 29 BCE

Chapter

4

Confucius

Confucius, one of the greatest thinkers in history, is most famous for founding the tradition-discipline named for him—Confucianism. Unlike Hinduism, Judaism, and Christianity, Confucianism is not a religion. Rather, it is a philosophy. As such, it is a way of seeing the world and of behaving in a humane and ethical way within society. A large portion of Confucian thinking and values deals with ethics and morality. So Confucianism is often considered and studied alongside the major religions, which also have strong ethical components.

Confucian thought and action is characterized in large degree by worldliness and secularism (non-spirituality). Many of the leading ancient religious figures, including the Buddha and Jesus, rejected worldly pursuits, lived in poverty, and preached about spirituality. Confucius was a very different sort of person and thinker. He spent much of his life as a civil servant and tried to create political and governmental reforms that would make society and its leaders more ethical and honest. His philosophy and distinctive approach to government inspired hundreds of millions of people over the centuries. So it would not be an exaggeration to say that he was one of the most influential people in human history.

A Turbulent Era

Confucius lived at the end of the so-called Spring and Autumn period of ancient China. The Zhou Dynasty came to power by overthrowing the Shang Dynasty. (A dynasty is a family line of rulers.) But in 771 BCE warlike outsiders sacked the Zhou court and killed its king. With the royal line broken, the power of the Zhou Dynasty collapsed. In the Spring and Autumn period that followed, China became a hodge-podge of mostly small, independent, and always competing kingdoms. This turbulent period was marked by political diversity, feudal rivalries, civil war, and bureaucratic (governmental) mismanagement.

In the kingdom of Lu, in northern China, where Confucius was born, there were three leading noble families. People born outside of these families had no hope of finding better jobs or otherwise improving their lives. Meanwhile, thieves roamed the streets, laws frequently went unheeded, and most people feared for their safety.

Yet despite its political and other uncertainties, the period was notable for a number of earnest attempts at governmental reform and new, constructive political ideas. Regional lords wanted to build strong armies, increase economic production, and develop

Confucius

Bratsk

Novosibirsk

Irkutsk

Ulaanbaatar

MONGOLIA

S I A

Urümqi

GOBI

STAN

Yumen

Yinchuan

Hoh

Be

CHINA

tan

Zhe

Xian

W

Chengdu

LHASA

SHUAN

Chongqing

Kunming

Guiyang

GLADESH

AMAR

Macau

cultural productivity. To this end, they built new weapons of war and improved farm equipment. They also dug canals, constructed irrigation systems, and built huge walls around the cities for protection from invaders.

As cultural life advanced, there was a need for skilled and literate diplomats, administrators, military advisors, and teachers. Many of the thinkers were traveling intellectuals who, besides teaching their students, were employed as advisors to state rulers on the methods of government, war, and diplomacy. Confucius was the best known of these traveling advisors.

A Fabled Birth

Confucius's father, Shuh-Liang Heih, had been a soldier who had gained the reputation of a hero who people everywhere looked up to. One day when he was getting on in age, a friend asked him why a soldier as widely honored as he seemed so sad. Shuh-Liang Heih answered that he was depressed because his wife had died. Also, together they had had nine daughters, but no son to carry on the family line.

The friend told Shuh-Liang Heih that the noble Yen family had three unmarried daughters. And any of the three would consider it an honor to marry such a highly regarded soldier and bear him a son. Hearing this, Shuh-Liang Heih decided to ask for one of Mr. Yen's daughters in marriage. And sure enough, one of them, Ching-tsai, agreed to marry Shuh-Liang Heih.

Nothing for certain is known about the birth and early childhood of the son born to Shuh-Liang Heih and Ching-tsai, other than his name, Confucius. However, a number of fables developed later. In one, the young bride dreamed that a spirit appeared and told her that she would have a son who would become wise beyond other men. In another story, the pregnant Ching-tsai had a vision in which five old men appeared. They were leading a strange creature with a horn growing from its forehead and scales like a reptile. Kneeling before Ching-tsai, the creature dropped a tablet of jade stone from its mouth and put its head in her lap. She realized that this was a good omen sent from the gods. On the jade stone was a message that said that her son would become a king without a throne.

These myths aside, Confucius was born in Lu in about 551 BCE. His parents named him K'ung Ch'iu. "Confucius" is a Latin form of K'ung-fu-tze. Meaning "K'ung the Master," it was a title of respect given to him as a grown-up philosopher and teacher by his closest followers.

A Diligent Worker

Confucius's father died when he was young. And his mother used the small amount of money her husband had left her to give her son a good education. Confucius loved school and would have liked to spend all his time studying the Chinese classics and playing the lute (a guitar-like instrument). Because his mother could not afford such luxury, he worked after school. He also found time for gymnastics, learning to drive a chariot, and studying traditional Chinese rituals.

At age seventeen, Confucius accepted a government job supervising grain storage. He kept records on bamboo strips and checked to make sure there were no mice or other vermin in the grain storage. "My calculations must be right," he said of his job. "That is all I have to care about." Soon he was promoted to the position of manager of state farm animals. In the fields, he was as conscientious as he was at keeping the books. He wrote, "The oxen and sheep must be fat and strong. That is all I have to care about."

When some of the herdsmen were quarreling over various issues, Confucius called them together. "Do not do to others what you do not wish [done to] yourself," he said. This a version of the famous and universal Golden Rule. Confucius felt that in applying it, people should repay kindness with kindness, but also repay evil with justice. Partly because he advocated such ethical concepts, the community came to greatly respect him. People sensed that he possessed a moral character beyond that of most other men.

Following Chinese custom, at age nineteen the young man chose a wife. And a year later she gave birth to a son. By now the state of Lu thought so highly of Confucius that the ruler, called a duke, gave him a present of two costly fish known as carp. Confucius was so pleased with this gift that he named the baby boy Li (meaning "the carp").

For five years Confucius worked diligently for the government and enjoyed life with his wife and son. Then, in about 527 BCE, his mother died. To pay final honor to her memory, Confucius followed ancient Chinese custom by retiring from his job for a period of two years.

Teaching About Right and Wrong

At the end of the two years, Confucius returned to public life as a teacher. His home became a meeting place where learned young men gathered to discuss governmental policy, philosophy, and especially moral concepts. In the evenings children from noble families came to Confucius with questions about right and wrong. And because his answers always appeared to be fair and correct, his reputation grew. People began to call him the "master teacher."

Confucius taught his students that a good or superior person always works hard to become better. The way we treat others, he pointed out, affects the quality of the society in which we live. If both a ruler and his subjects are immoral, their society will be corrupt and disordered. Conversely, if a ruler and his people act ethically, their society will be constructive and well-ordered.

When a priest asked him about his views on heaven, Confucius replied, "Sincerity is the way of heaven [and] he who [acts sincerely] is he who chooses what is good and firmly holds it fast." Sincerity and truthfulness were concepts he strongly stressed with his students. Again and again he told them if they were genuine and honest in all their actions, everything would go well for them.

Another area in which Confucius proved to be a master was lute-playing. He advocated that music could be used to foster good government. The right kind of music should stir up the goodness in men's minds, he said, and put a stop to most evil thoughts and feelings. He did not believe it possible for a good musician to be a mean or bad person. But not all music was beneficial, he added. Some could be harmful to the character and even to society. "By hearing the music sanctioned by a ruler," he wrote, "one may judge of his virtue."

In the year 518 BCE, when Confucius was thirty-three years old, news of his great knowledge reached one of Lu's chief government administrators, Meng-xi. As the latter lay on his deathbed,

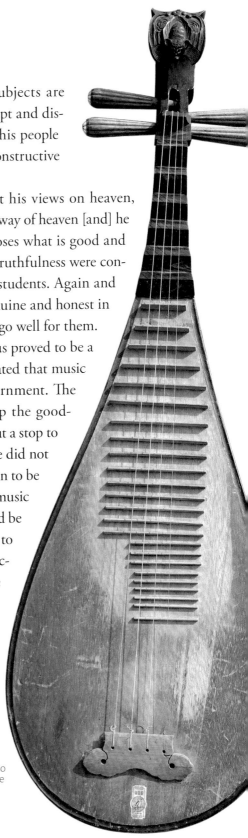

A four-stringed *pipa*, also known as a Chinese lute

he urged his son to study under Confucius. The son did as his father requested, but confessed to Confucius that he was afraid he would not be able to serve as well as his father had. Confucius advised him to look into his own heart and if he found nothing wrong there, then there was nothing to fear. He would be a noble official or ruler.

Confucius's fame as a great philosopher-teacher steadily increased. He opened his house not only to the sons of nobles but also to the poorest young men in the land. He took payment from those who could afford it. Others he taught for free, as long as they were hard-working, sincere, and honest. He also expected them to be very self-disciplined, just as he himself was. "I do not open up the truth to one who is not eager to get knowledge," he told them, "nor help out anyone who is not anxious to explain himself."

One student complained that some of the ethical problems Confucius presented were so complex that he could not figure them out. The master teacher replied, "When you know a thing [and] recognize that you know it, and when you do not [know it and admit] that you do not know—that is [true] knowledge."

Traveling with His Students

At some point late in 518 or early in 517 BCE, Confucius decided to leave his home and travel to some neighboring kingdoms. He had a small oxcart and invited his students to go with him if they wished. Some of the students did accompany him. The ox walked slowly, and as the students walked along beside the cart Confucius led discussions with them. One day a student complained that some of Confucius's students were unworthy of him. Confucius replied, "When you see an admirable person, think of emulating [copying] him; when you see one who is not so, turn inward and examine yourself."

Eventually Confucius and his students reached the kingdom of Lo. There, according to some ancient accounts, he met Lao Tzu, the Taoist master of wisdom. (Taoism, pronounced DOW-is-um, is a Chinese religion-philosophy that explores the relationship between humanity and nature and the universe.) The old sage seemed somewhat critical of Confucius's approach to philosophy, saying that it placed too much emphasis on politics and worldly affairs. Confucius countered that human society badly needed wise, humane political leaders. And he pointed out that it was the duty of philosophers to teach the leaders to do their jobs well. But Lao Tzu said that wise men should stay away from public employment and not share their intellectual assets with anyone, including politicians.

Most modern scholars think that this meeting between the two great Chinese thinkers never happened. Like so many other stories later invented about great men and women, this one seems contrived. In any case, there is no credible evidence that the two men ever met.

More credible were some other incidents that supposedly occurred while Confucius was staying in Lo. The story goes that he walked over some grounds where ancient sacrifices had taken place. He also visited the Hall of Light, a structure erected by one of the past emperors to give audiences to foreign dignitaries. When a student said that there did not seem to be anything to learn from the hall, Confucius informed him that one must study the past to understand the present.

As an example, he pointed to an old wooden bucket and explained that it was once a symbol of good government. When a student asked why, Confucius carried the bucket to a fountain. He dipped the bucket in the water to show the student that when the bucket had too much water in it, it would sink to the bottom. When it had too little water, however, it floated uselessly.

The bucket was a parable of good government, he said. For rulers to go too far was as bad as their falling too short.

On his way home from Lo, Confucius's fame went before him and many people he met along the road recognized his name. Students from several villages rushed out to meet the master and begged him to offer them some wisdom as he passed through. These and other students later recorded his short sayings in a book called *The Analects* (from Greek words meaning "things gathered").

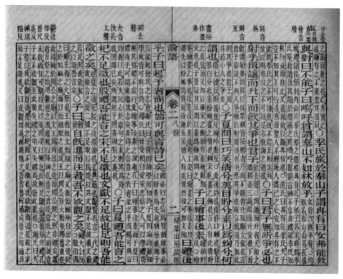

The Analects of Confucius were written by
his disciples thirty to fifty years after his death.

Confucius Meets Duke Ching

Shortly after Confucius returned home to Lu in 517 BCE, civil strife broke out. Opponents of the ruler, Duke Chao, who was also Confucius's friend, forced Chao to flee the country. Confucius decided to go along with the duke into exile in the neighboring kingdom of Ch'i.

On the way to Ch'i, Chao's party encountered a woman weeping beside a grave. Concerned, Confucius stopped his oxcart and asked why she was crying. She explained that at that very place a tiger had killed her husband's father. Soon after that, a tiger had killed her husband, and now her son, too, had been slain by a tiger. Confucius asked the woman if she had considered moving to a safer place where there were no tigers. She told him that although the tigers in the region were fierce, the government was honest and helped the people. In contrast, the governments of the tiger-free states were corrupt and exploited their peoples. Confucius saw this as a teachable moment. "Mark this well," he told his students, who had also accompanied the duke. "Oppressive government is fiercer than a tiger."

In Ch'i, Duke Chao took refuge with that kingdom's leader, Duke Ching. When Ching heard that the famous Confucius was in his city, he sent a messenger to bring the great teacher to his court. On his arrival, the duke questioned Confucius about his opinion of government. Confucius replied, "There is government when the prince is a prince, and the minister is a minister [and] when the father is a father, and the son is a son." He informed the duke that good government occurs when each political office has its logical place and when each official does not take on the duty of another. Fascinated, the duke questioned him further and Confucius said, "To govern means to rectify [make things better]. If you lead the people with correctness [and thereby set a good example], who [among them] will dare not to be correct?"

Confucius also advised the duke that for a government to work for the betterment of all, its members should frequently check on the people's needs, always be honest, and whenever possible go with the dictates of their hearts. Also, a country's leaders should make their family life orderly and efficient; only then can they likewise make the government orderly and efficient.

Impressed, the duke asked Confucius to stay on as his advisor. But one of the duke's existing advisors, who was clearly jealous of Confucius, took the duke aside and argued against hiring a scholar who thought he knew everything. Such a man might soon want to run the government himself, the advisor warned. Duke Ching pondered his advisor's words and then told Confucius that he was too old to learn so many new ideas. He now offered Confucius some extensive local lands, the revenues from which would provide the philosopher a hefty income.

But Confucius declined this offer. For him, an honorable man should take monetary rewards only for services performed. He had given the duke advice on good government and he had rejected it. The offer of revenues from the lands was therefore unacceptable. It was clear to Confucius that Duke Ching did not understand him very well.

Calling for Better Education

Confucius and his students eventually returned to Lu. And for the next fifteen years he taught them and others, including his son. He also researched the disciplines of art, poetry, music, history, and traditional Chinese customs. To be fully human, he said, one must love art. Art has the power to transform human nature by making it more virtuous, he declared. Moreover, any nation that educated its young people in art, poetry, music, and dance would quickly prove itself superior to other nations. The leaders of those nations would then have no choice but to make their own governments and educational systems like those of the superior one. That way, over time the whole world would become better.

Better educational systems would take advantage of the good qualities people already have, Confucius argued. In fact, he

A Ming Dynasty illustration of Confucius with his students

believed that human beings are by their very natures good. So if government officials treat people in an ethical manner, people will treat one another the same way. It is crucial, he said, for a society to practice ethical values in all they think and do. Mothers and fathers, and even kings and princes, should live their lives so as to be moral examples to their families and nations. Thus, setting an example is more important than speaking words. And for a society to achieve harmony, each person must be ethical.

To inspire people to be ethical, Confucius taught, schools must actually teach moral values, or virtues. The Five Cardinal Virtues, he proposed, are Jen, Chun-tzu, Li, Te, and Wen. Jen is the ideal relationship between two people, in which they develop deep feelings of respect for each other. Because they learn to be unselfish, they come to see all people as brothers and sisters. Chun-tzu, said Confucius, is the "superior person," who treats others with justice and love. In societies that lack Chun-tzu, he warned, war is inevitable. Li is the mean, or proper balance, between two extremes in moral conduct, both within the family and within society. When politicians and other leaders achieve that balance, they can create Te, consisting of guidelines for honest, just government. Finally, Confucius said, Wen is the state of peace and contentment found in the arts, music, and philosophy. Art has the power to guide human beings toward the good.

A Series of Promotions

Confucius realized that it would be easier for him to effectively introduce his educational proposals and other ethical values into government if he served in a high government post. He was pleased, therefore, when in 501 BCE he was appointed chief magistrate (administrator) of the city of Chung-tu. Confucius threw himself into his work. In his view, the position of magistrate was like the father of a large family in which nothing was too small or too large for his attention. First, he made sure that no citizen went hungry. He also honored the dead and urged people to act ethically at all times. It was clear that he respected the people, and seeing him as a role model, many of them began to show more respect for each other than they had in the past. As a result, petty crimes such as stealing ceased. In addition, the people showed more respect for the land. Following Confucius's advice, they started employing farming techniques that conserved water more efficiently than older methods had.

Confucius was also pleased to see his ideas spread to neighboring towns and cities. Impressed with the progress made in Chung-tu, they adopted the same ideas and methods and applied them to their own situations. Lu's highest government officials were also impressed. They promoted Confucius to the post of assistant superintendent of works. And not long afterward he acquired the important position of minister of crime.

In his newest job, Confucius studied the prisons and investigated the prisoners' records. Then he called together all the judges and lawyers, along with his own assistants. He informed them that his study of the prisons had shown that most of the inmates were poor and ignorant people. By educating the people in useful trades and occupations, he said, they could greatly decrease the amount of poverty and ignorance in society and thereby significantly reduce the prison population.

Another example of the wisdom Confucius displayed while serving as minister of crime occurred when a father charged his own son with disobeying him and getting into trouble. Confucius promptly put them both in prison for three months. When he released them, some observers argued that Confucius should have had the disrespectful son executed rather than imprisoning the guiltless father. But Confucius said that the father was *not* guiltless. He explained that the father had not set a good example, and that was why the son was disobedient. Thus, it was as much the father's crime as it was the son's.

A Wicked Scheme

Confucius was so effective in his job that he eventually became prime minister of Lu. For the first time in Chinese history, a mutual respect grew up between a government and the people it ruled. But when Lu blossomed into a rich and influential state, some princes and rulers in neighboring kingdoms grew anxious. They not only envied Lu's success, but also feared that it might attack and absorb them.

For this reason, the leader of the kingdom of T'si devised a scheme for sowing discord between Confucius and the duke who ruled Lu. With the aid of some other foreign leaders who worried about Lu's growing influence, the leader of T'si took advantage of the duke's weakness for women and horses. They chose eighty beautiful girls skilled in art, music, and dancing. They also selected 120 of the finest horses in China, and they sent the women and horses as gifts to the duke of Lu.

The duke of Lu was thrilled to receive these gifts. Just as the foreign leaders had anticipated, he rapidly shifted his attention to the women and horses. And as he did so, he neglected most of his governmental duties. He also refused Confucius's counsel, which was to pay more attention to his job as ruler. It was almost time for the most important state ceremony of the year, called the Sacrifice to Heaven. Confucius hoped that the need to plan for this occasion would bring the duke to his senses. But the duke showed no interest. Not only did he omit some important rituals and hurry through others, he eventually got up and left in the middle of the festivities.

As the duke neglected more and more of his duties, the government grew increasingly less effective. In disgust, and realizing that it was not his place to perform the duke's duties for him, Confucius resigned. At age fifty-six, he gathered some of his crestfallen students and traveled westward to the state of Wei. When the group arrived at the border of Wei, Confucius tried to cheer up his followers. He told them that it might take a long time, but eventually peoples and nations would successfully implement his teachings.

What Confucius and his students did not know was that the leader of Wei had been a partner in the wicked scheme to ruin both Confucius and Lu's government. The leader of Wei tried to get on Confucius's good side by offering him enough grain to support him for the rest of his life. But Confucius refused this offer. He left Wei and began traveling from place to place, teaching and lecturing for a while at each stop.

A Genuinely Good Man

After thirteen years of wandering, Confucius finally returned to his native state of Lu. There he taught, wrote a history of Lu, and collected old Chinese poetry. When he reached the age of seventy, his son, Li, died. And Li's own son, Keigh, came to live with his grandfather. Confucius became convinced that the young man would do a good job of carrying on his work and teachings.

In Confucius's seventy-second year, he gathered together his closest followers. "No intelligent monarch arises," he told them with a touch of sadness. "There is not one in the empire that will make me his master [teacher]. My time has come to die." That night Confucius went to bed early and seven days later he died. The year was 479 BCE.

Although Confucius never considered himself to be the founder of a religion, some people did come to worship him, or at least his memory. His fame continued to spread. And over time his ideas came to be used in the training of all government officials. He became so highly respected that in 195 BCE a Chinese emperor visited his tomb and offered sacrifices. Soon other emperors built shrines honoring Confucius. Even many centuries later when China was no longer an empire, his ethical ideals continued to be taught in Chinese schools. In this way, enormous numbers of people over many generations and centuries came to benefit from the tireless work of a genuinely good man.

The Taiwan Confucian Temple in Taipei, built in the late seventeenth century

A painting of Zoroaster on display in the Ateshkadeh Zoroastrian temple in the Iranian city of Yazd

Chapter

5

Zoroaster

The prophet Zoroaster was the founder of Zoroastrianism, a religion first practiced in ancient Persia, what is now Iran and some neighboring regions. The name Zoroaster is derived from Zoroastres, a Latin variant of the Iranian name Zarathushtra. He was known to the ancient Greeks and Romans as Zoroaster. The Persians called him Zartosht.

Zoroaster may have been the world's first monotheist, or believer in a single god. Before he arrived on the scene, the vast majority of people in Persia, the rest of the Middle East, and other parts of the world were polytheistic. That is, they believed

An 1814 map of Persia

in and worshiped multiple gods. (The ancient Jews were also monotheistic, as was the Egyptian pharaoh Akhenaten; but it remains unclear who came first: the Jews, Akhenaten, or Zoroaster.)

Polytheists carved images of gods from stone and molded them out of clay. Some people worshiped birds and beasts as gods. Animal blood and various plants and liquids flowed on their altars as sacrifices (offerings) to these deities.

This changed, in Persia at least, during the late second millennium or early first millennium BCE. The traditional, very ancient polytheist faith practiced in Iran was for the most part replaced by Zoroastrianism. That religion holds that there is only one God—Ahura Mazda—often called the "Wise Lord."

Zoroastrianism survived through numerous wars and rising and falling empires and for almost a thousand years was one of the most popular religions in the Middle East. Some modern scholars think that Zoroastrian theology and cosmology (explanations for the universe and humanity's place within it) may have influenced the development of Jewish, Christian, and Muslim thought. Due to large-scale invasions by the Arabs and Alexander the Great, however, Iran's vast ancient libraries were destroyed. So extremely few reliable sources describing original Zoroastrian theology have survived.

Likewise, almost nothing for certain is known about when Zoroaster lived and the events of his life. A number of legends and third-hand accounts by ancient Greek writers have survived. And modern historians must do their best, using archaeology and other means, to estimate which parts of these writings might be at least partially based in fact.

A Divinely Inspired Birth

The thorny matter of Zoroaster's birth is a good example of this continuing uncertainty. Ancient Greek and Roman writers thought he was born around 6000 BCE, more than 5,000 years before their own era. But modern historians have shown that this is far too early. A few later ancient and early modern writers suggested that he lived in the 600s BCE, shortly before the founding of the Persian Empire by King Cyrus II. This has also been shown to be incorrect. More recent linguistic studies of early Zoroastrian writings indicate that the faith's founder was born earlier than 900 BCE, but *not* earlier than 1700 BCE. And the world's leading expert on Zoroaster and his religion, University of London scholar Mary Boyce, favors the middle ground; she thinks that Zoroaster lived sometime between 1400 and 1000 BCE.

Whenever Zoroaster's birth date actually was, the legends say that his father, Porushasp Spitama, was a member of an important Iranian warrior clan. Also, his mother, Dughdova, was supposedly from a noble family. They lived in a town west of the Caspian Sea. While Dughdova was with child, the story goes, magicians read signs that the unborn baby would be a holy and influential prophet and teacher. To prevent the birth of such a child, who might end up competing with them, the magicians decided to kill the baby before he was born.

The method the magicians chose must have been poison because Dughdova suddenly began suffering from terrible stomach cramps. She doubled over in pain and fever raged through her body until she lay near death. To find the cause of her illness, Porushasp Spitama called for some local doctors. But the voice of an angel suddenly appeared and told Dughdova not to listen to these physicians. Any medicine they gave her, the angel said, might harm the special child she was carrying. Dughdova asked the angel what she could do to survive her ordeal and get better. The angel instructed her to wash her hands and then take wood and make a fire. If she offered cow butter to the purifying fire, she would get well. The desperate woman did as the angel said and her health immediately improved.

As the tale of Zoroaster's birth continues, for three nights beforehand a ray of light illumined the village where his father and mother lived. Seeing this seemingly miraculous vision, the local inhabitants were certain that the child would be a blessing from the gods. When Zoroaster was born, legend claims, he laughed. The midwives helping his mother had never heard a child laugh when he was born. So they agreed that it must be another sign that the birth was divinely inspired.

Meanwhile, the magicians worried that Zoroaster had come to Earth to destroy the shrines and idols that the Iranians worshiped and to banish the magicians from the land. Once more, they conspired to kill him. Zoroaster's father learned of the plot and challenged the magicians to try harming a child who was under divine protection. The chief magician suddenly grabbed the baby from his father's arms and threw him in front of a herd of stampeding oxen. Immediately the lead ox stood over the baby, protecting it while the rest of the herd thundered by.

Deciding on still another murderous plan, the magicians lit a blazing fire on a temple altar. When Zoroaster's mother passed by, they snatched the child from her and threw him into the fire.

A chromolithograph of the birth of Zoroaster, from a 1936 postcard series

While they waited for the fire to consume the boy, Zoroaster calmly sat inside the blaze, laughing and playing with the flames.

Next, the magicians decided to feed Zoroaster to the wolves. While the wolves were out hunting, the magicians abducted the boy from his home and carried him into the wolves' den. When the wolves returned, to the magicians' surprise, the creatures formed a circle of protection around the child. At dawn an angel led Zoroaster's mother to the wolves' den. There she blessed the wolves, cradled the child in her arms, and took him home. Unable to think of any other way to kill an infant who was clearly under divine protection, the magicians gave up.

Compassion for all Creatures

As a growing boy, the legends claim, Zoroaster was wise beyond his years. Although he had the body of a child, he had the mind of a genius and the visions of a saint. One day he gazed upward, downward, and to his side. When his father asked him what he saw, Zoroaster said that when he looked upward, he saw good souls going to heaven; looking downward, he saw a demon; and to his side he saw people whom the god Ahura Mazda had clothed in fine robes.

As a child Zoroaster spent much of his time alone in nature with the wild animals. Studying the natural world, he learned about life and death and joy and pain. He asked his parents why there had to be both good and evil instead of only good. Of course, they did not know how to answer him.

When the boy was seven, his parents sent him to study under Burzin-Kurus, a teacher of wisdom known throughout ancient Persia. In Zoroaster the teacher saw a prophet destined to teach and lead people to greater understanding. Burzin-Kurus informed Porushasp and Dughdova that their son had come into the world with a great amount of knowledge and love. He advised them that the child had an understanding of certain divine mysteries and unconditional compassion for all creatures.

After studying with Burzin-Kurus for eight years, Zoroaster returned home to work with his brothers on his father's farm. He was fifteen when his four brothers approached him to divide the family's property among themselves. Zoroaster took only one item, an object used in religious rituals, and left everything else to his brothers.

It was while he was working on the farm that Zoroaster heard the news that a foreign army had invaded Persia. That very day he left home, intending to go into the battlefield and treat wounded soldiers. The doctors on the front lines of the war were impressed with him and called him a skilled healer.

Visit from an Angel

When he was twenty, Zoroaster left his parents to go on a quest for life's hidden truths. To that lofty aim, he first journeyed into the desert and climbed into a mountain cave. There he stayed for a while and meditated and prayed, hoping this approach would reveal the truths he sought. Weeks became months, which in turn became years. For ten years Zoroaster lived in the desolate mountains, repeatedly praying to Ahura Mazda to reveal the meaning of life and death and right and wrong. Supposedly (according to legendary accounts), he experienced long periods of discouragement, hunger, and doubt. Voices sometimes tempted him, urging him to give up and return to his family and friends. But he closed his ears to these voices and continued his life of solitude and privation.

Zoroaster also continued to pray to Ahura Mazda, begging him to appear and teach him the great truths. "Speak to me as friend to friend," the young man implored. "Grant us the support which friend would give to friend."

When he reached the age of thirty, Zoroaster suddenly had a major and overpowering revelation. It seemed as though the presence and power of God had materialized both inside and outside of his quaking body. The area in which he was standing abruptly became illuminated by a bright light. And Vohu Mana, the angel of Good Thought, appeared. The being, who was as tall as three

Zoroaster, a 1931 oil painting by Nicholas Roerich

spears and carrying a twig in his hand as a sign of peace, asked Zoroaster what he desired. The man replied, "I am Zoroaster of the Spitamas. Righteousness is my chief desire, and my wish is to know and do the will of the sacred beings, as they show me."

Instead of giving a verbal answer, Vohu Mana took Zoroaster on a journey. For each nine steps taken by the angel, Zoroaster had to take ninety steps. Eventually they entered the beautiful domain of the angels, where no shadow could be seen. Vohu Mana told Zoroaster that he could now ask again about the object of his quest.

Nature's Opposing Forces

Zoroaster asked how God had accomplished the creation and was told that the Wise Lord had created all that exists in seven stages. Through his Holy Spirit (Spenta Mainyu), Ahura Mazda had fashioned six spirit-divinities called the Immortal Holy Ones, who had helped the Wise Lord create the world. When Zoroaster asked the angel to explain further, he was told that each of the six divinities had a special characteristic of the all-good Ahura Mazda. One had Good Thought, another Righteousness, and the others had Power, Devotion, Health, and Long Life, respectively. These were qualities that people could also possess, the angel said. So the six spirits in a sense bridged the gap between humans and God.

A chromolithograph of Zoroaster bearing fire and law, and guided by an angel, from a 1936 postcard series

Zoroaster next asked about the nature of God. And the angel deferred to God, allowing the great Ahura Mazda to speak for himself. The Wise Lord revealed to Zoroaster that he was composed of eternal light. His spiritual fire purified the soul and consumed all that was not clean, he explained. On Earth, the closest element to this spiritual light was fire. So those who kept the eternal flame burning were seen by God as good people. As a test of Zoroaster's faith, Ahura Mazda had him walk through fire, which he did without suffering any burns.

Zoroaster now asked what one must do to become perfect. The Wise Lord explained that good thoughts, good words, and good deeds were the three so-called perfections. To lead a truly good life, he said, people must carefully control their thoughts, their words, and their actions.

Ahura Mazda went on to tell Zoroaster that an evil spirit named Ahriman opposed the Wise Lord. As a result, God and the wicked Ahriman were continually at war with each other. Their respective supporters—for Ahura Mazda called Asa, or the Truth, and for Ahriman called Drug (pronounced *droog*), or the Lie—also constantly opposed each other. The physical world, Zoroaster learned, had a dual nature. That is, it was characterized by couplets, or groups of two opposing things or concepts, each of which mirrored the larger battle between Ahura Mazda and Ahriman and between the Truth and the Lie. Among these couplets were day and night; pleasure and pain; light and darkness; truth and falsehood; and life and death. Human beings were free to choose between the way of truth and the way of evil. Good people were honest, kind, and understanding, whereas evil people were proud, dishonest, and deceitful.

Zoroaster asked what happened when someone died and was told that at death each soul was judged according to its goodness and commitment to a life of goodness. After this judgment, the soul could choose either to enter Ahriman's repulsive realm (essentially hell) or the heavenly realm of Ahura Mazda. Before entering one of these realms, the soul of the dead person had to cross the Chinvat Bridge. This extended from heaven to hell. Here the soul could read its own past life record. If good deeds triumphed over evil deeds in that life, the soul could look toward paradise. But if evil triumphed over good, the soul was condemned to the awful abyss below the bridge.

Ahura Mazda then took Zoroaster to higher levels of consciousness, beyond all dualities, and commanded him to become a prophet of the Wise Lord. His task was to teach humankind about goodness and truth. Those who loved light, truth, and honesty would live in heavenly light forever; while those who preferred evil, lies, and darkness would, appropriately, live eternally in darkness.

Standing Up to Evil

Awed and transformed by the wonders he had experienced in the heavens, Zoroaster returned to Earth. He was ready to begin his ministry—to teach humans about the truth of Ahura Mazda and how to attain lives of goodness. The man came down from the cave that had been his home for ten years.

On the first night of Zoroaster's journey home, a demon in the form of a beautiful woman came to tempt him. She told him she was a goddess. But Zoroaster ordered her to turn around. He knew that if the woman was as beautiful behind as she was in front, there was a chance she was telling the truth. She tried to resist, but the power in his words compelled her to turn around, and sure enough, her back was a mass of serpents, toads, lizards, and centipedes. Zoroaster commanded her to leave and again she felt forced to obey. According to legend, news of his first triumph over evil echoed throughout the heavens.

On the second night after Zoroaster's return, the evil Ahriman came to him and promised that together they could control all people. The Lord of Evil, as Ahriman was sometimes called, guaranteed that if the man left the good religion of Ahura Mazda he would make him the ruler of nations. They would inspire people to seek material power, or imprison them in guilt and despair. People could not keep their hearts turned to God, Ahriman said, when offered huge amounts of money and power.

But the newly appointed prophet stood firm. "Even should my body be torn, [I] will [not] renounce the good religion," he proclaimed. Zoroaster said that he was on Earth to teach people about the good life and to guide them on the path of righteousness and away from temptation. Challenging Zoroaster, Ahriman asked what weapons he thought he could use to combat the Lord of Evil. And Zoroaster answered: "With the sacred mortar, with the sacred cup, with the Word proclaimed by [Ahura]

Mazda, with my own weapon, and it is the best one. With this Word will I vanquish [you], with this Word will I withstand [you], with this weapon will the good creatures withstand and vanquish you, O malignant [hateful] Ahriman !"

The next day Zoroaster arrived at his parents' house. From there he set about teaching people the good life, but at first his words offended them. The problem was that most of them were not as spiritual as he had recently become. Just as the demon had said, their main interests were money, pleasure, and power. They preferred to worship idols, which they could see, rather than an invisible god they could *not* see. As a result, they refused to listen to Zoroaster.

Yet the prophet persevered. He praised and sang hymns to the Wise Lord. He also taught that each person was free to choose his or her own creed. And when people asked him why they should believe him, he told them to examine their hearts and follow the inner light that existed in all of them. He urged them to be kind to all creatures. When a farmer asked him about the care of cattle, Zoroaster told him that a wicked man should not have animals. Cattle need to live in a pleasant place with grain and green pastures, the prophet said. Then a man asked him about dogs and Zoroaster said that a dog was a good creature loved by Ahura Mazda. If anyone should hit a dog or otherwise treat it cruelly, God would make sure he paid for the crime.

The First Disciple

Unfortunately for Zoroaster, most of these teachings fell on deaf ears. In fact, even after the passage of ten years the prophet had gained no converts to his faith. Feeling as though he could not fulfill his mission, Zoroaster asked the Wise Lord: "To what land shall I bend my steps? Where shall I turn?" He complained that most human rulers were "cruel despots" and "followers of the Lie." How, then, Zoroaster asked, could he please the mighty Ahura Mazda?

According to legend, the Wise Lord helped the prophet by inspiring Zoroaster's cousin, Maedyoimaha, to become his first follower. Maedyoimaha asked his cousin if the earth people walked on was sacred and he told him that everything in nature was sacred. But Maedyoimaha insisted that this could not be true. How could earth be sacred if it was contaminated by the dead bodies buried in it? Zoroaster explained that in the religion of Ahura Mazda, dead bodies would be placed in "towers of silence," wooden frameworks, where the birds could pick the bones clean of decaying flesh. In that way, the bodies would give life to other creatures and not contaminate the ground.

One day Maedyoimaha suggested that the new teachings might be too difficult to understand for the uneducated peasants, who found it easier to hold onto the old ways. It might be easier, he said, if the teachings were first aimed at educated upper-class people, including the king, his nobles, and the members of the priestly class.

Winning Over a King

Zoroaster agreed. He and his disciple traveled to the Persian king's palace and asked to see the reigning monarch, King Vishtaspa. The palace guards curtly informed them that the king did not give audiences to lowly beggars. Instead of objecting, Zoroaster simply thanked the guard and walked away. Each day for six days the prophet returned to the palace and asked to see the king. And each day the guards turned him away.

On the seventh day, however, Zoroaster stood before the guards and commanded them to tell King Vishtaspa that he had come to tell him about great truths. One guard asked him who he was.

Zoroaster, educating and reforming the people, as depicted in a 1936 chromolithograph

And he answered that he was the prophet of Ahura Mazda, the Wise Lord. Hearing this, the guard pulled out his sword as if to slay Zoroaster. But the latter instantly created a ball of fire and held the burning flame in the palm of his hand. Awestruck, the guard dropped his sword and ran inside the palace. And soon the king granted Zoroaster the audience he had requested.

The king also invited several magicians, priests, and philosophers to listen to and question Zoroaster about the new religion. The first question came from the king himself. He asked if Zoroaster had come to preach against the idols that most people worshiped. Zoroaster answered that he had not come to condemn anyone or anything; instead, he had come to preach the great truths of Ahura Mazda, the one true god.

The magicians, priests, and philosophers then began to question Zoroaster while the king listened. For three days, the legendary accounts say, a spirited debate ensued. Through it all Zoroaster's voice carried the power and depth of a mighty ocean. He answered the magicians, philosophers, and priests in a kind manner but with tremendous authority. When they asked him about the one true god, Zoroaster explained that Ahura Mazda bestowed light and intelligence on the world. So he had chosen as his symbol a wondrous manifestation of light—namely fire. Moreover, God had created the sun, the Earth, the stars, the moon, the animals, the plants, and the sky. Greater than all the rest, however, the Wise Lord had created humans, whom he desired to be righteous like himself.

Then they challenged Zoroaster to define a righteous person. He answered that a righteous person was one who had good thoughts, good words, and good deeds. Righteousness, he added, was also the quality that stayed with the soul after death.

Trying to stump the prophet, the priests asked what humanity's mission on Earth was. He answered that people had been placed on Earth to learn about the struggle between good and evil, between God and the evil Ahriman. They could then choose good over evil and thereby raise humanity's standing, both in the present world and in the life to come in heaven. If they instead chose evil over good, he said, they would end up in hell.

The king's guests also questioned Zoroaster about worship and animal sacrifices. He told them that a good deed was superior to ten thousand prayers. Animals, he said, were under the protection of the Wise Lord. So those who gave animals food, protection, and love were nearer to God than those who did not.

By the end of the third day, having heard all the arguments, King Vishtaspa had become convinced that Zoroaster spoke the truth. The monarch publicly embraced the new teachings. He also appointed Zoroaster high priest and told the royal family, the nobles, and all the public officials to accept the prophet's teachings. News of the new religion spread throughout the land and soon many ordinary people accepted the divinely inspired messages Zoroaster had brought.

His Ideas Lived On

Not long after the king accepted the new faith, he ordered his scribes to write down in letters of gold all of the prophet's teachings. Collectively, these became known as the *Avesta*. And thereafter it was seen as the sacred scripture of the Zoroastrian religion.

Zoroaster now had numerous disciples, some of whom traveled to neighboring kingdoms to spread the message of the greatness of the one true god, Ahura Mazda. They went to Palestine and Greece in the west and to India in the east. Their work was often difficult, as foreign armies attacked the Persian

Zoroastrians for what they saw as strange monotheistic beliefs. Great wars and battles occurred over the course of many years. In the end, Persia was victorious and Zoroaster became a hero to large numbers of people.

However, some foreigners remained opposed to Zoroaster and his new beliefs. And they continued to plot against him. When he was seventy-seven, some assassins found him kneeling in prayer before a sacred fire. Before he saw them, they rushed at him and stabbed him to death.

But though the prophet was dead, the ideas he preached lived on. His teachings continued to spread near and far. And more and more people came to believe that Ahura Mazda was the one true god and the creator of life and goodness. In this way, Zoroastrianism became the principal faith in all parts of the Persian Empire.

As the centuries wore on, however, various wars, conquests, and other obstacles threatened to annihilate that faith. These included the conquest of Persia by the Macedonian Greek king, Alexander the Great, in the late 300s BCE; a large-scale invasion by Arab Muslims in the 600s CE; and competition from other religious traditions, including Hinduism, Buddhism, Islam, and Christianity.

Yet just as Zoroaster himself had done centuries before, followers of the faith persevered. And today as many as a quarter of a million people still follow a somewhat modernized version of Zoroastrianism. Most of them dwell in India and Iran, but some live in other countries and continents. At least 4,000 reside in Britain alone. They and others who revere Zoroaster's memory hope that new insights into their belief system will help keep what may have been the first monotheistic religion alive and well for centuries to come.

Zoroaster's death in the fire temple, a place of worship for Zoroastrians. Zoraster's death is not mentioned in the *Avesta*, but in the Persian epic *Shah-nama*, he is said to have been killed at the alter during the invasion of Balkh, the home of Zoroastrianism. This depiction is one in a series of 1936 postcards commissioned by the Liebig's Extract and Meat Company

Chapter

6

Jesus

Christianity, the world's largest single faith, was born within the vast ethnic, cultural, and religious melting pot of the ancient Greco-Roman world. More specifically, the early Christians arose in a section of Palestine—Judea, which occupied what is now Israel and parts of Jordan. The Romans seized control of Judea in 63 BCE and made its rulers Roman clients. Such rulers, including many in Greece and elsewhere in Europe as well as in Palestine, were allowed to maintain control of their peoples. But they had to do Rome's bidding in larger affairs.

Later, in 6 CE, Rome did away with the client relationship with Judea and ruled it more directly, as a province of the

A Victorian map of Palestine

Roman Empire. At the time it made up only a tiny part of the vast Roman realm. By 4 BCE, the year Jesus was born (as estimated by modern scholars), about one out of every five people on Earth lived and died under Roman law.

Most Roman citizens readily accepted that system of laws and were quite content to be in charge of the known world. However, many of the peoples Rome had conquered to amass its huge realm were not nearly so happy. They resented paying whatever taxes the Romans decided to levy on them. They also disliked waking up each day to see Roman soldiers occupying their lands and cities. Some fervently longed for the day when they might reassert their independence and self-rule. And none among these peoples were more discontented and anti-Roman in outlook than the Jews, who made up most of Judea's population.

The Jews, from whose ranks the first Christians came, especially hated Judea's government. For a while they had a Jewish king, Herod. Also, their supreme local law court, the Sanhedrin, was made up of Jews. But Herod was little more than a pro-Roman puppet ruler who often brutalized his own people while enriching himself and living in luxury. And the members of the Sanhedrin were mainly upper-class Jews who benefited from maintaining the status quo and feared angering their Roman masters.

Those Jews who were willing to risk antagonizing Herod, and after his death the Sanhedrin, were members of society's lower classes. It was from their ranks that Jesus and his first followers came.

The Predicted Messiah

One initial difference between Jesus and his followers and the mainstream of Jewish society was that they believed that God's Kingdom was imminent. All Jews of that era believed in the coming of the Messiah, or "Anointed One." According to prophecy, the Messiah was a God-sent and powerful person or being who would come to free the Jews from subjugation by the Romans and others. According to the English writer Andrew N. Wilson, author of *Jesus: A Life* and *Paul: The Mind of the Apostle*:

> The Messiah would come down from the clouds in the likeness of the Son of man in the Book of Daniel. He would establish a kingdom which was an everlasting kingdom, having first crushed the [Jews'] enemies under his feet. The old temple of [the biblical king] Solomon would be restored in Jerusalem. [And] the Gentiles [non-Jews] would worship the god of Israel.

Most Jews assumed that the Messiah would come at some undetermined time in the future. Hopefully it would be in the next century or two, but they realized it might be even later. A minority of Jews, however, felt that the coming of God's Kingdom would likely take place much sooner—at any moment, or at least within their own lifetimes. In fact, a small band of Jews came to believe that Jesus himself was the predicted Messiah.

The Gospels

More is known about Jesus's teachings than the events of his life. This is because the principal ancient sources for Jesus say almost nothing about what he did from infancy to his late twenties. Those sources are known as the Gospels, a term meaning "good news." Titled Matthew, Mark, Luke, and John, they are the first four books of the New Testament. Together, the New Testament and Old Testament make up the Christian Bible. The only aspects of Jesus's life significantly covered by the Gospels are his birth, his ministry (preaching), his arrest by the authorities in Jerusalem, and his execution by the Romans.

Unfortunately for those who would like to know more about Jesus, even those parts of his life described in the Gospels are the subject of constant debate by historians and biblical scholars. The four documents were penned many years after Jesus's death. The result, many scholars point out, is that some sections might be factual, or nearly so, while others may be exaggerated or even fabricated. And it is difficult to know which sections are most reliable.

Nevertheless, the Gospels are indispensable because they contain the most widely accepted, or what might be termed "official," story of Jesus's life and deeds. Historians and other experts try to separate the facts from what they view as fiction, namely the miracles and other supernatural events. Meanwhile, many devout Christians accept the latter events as fact. They make the point that such things cannot be disproved any more than they can be proved, and so they believe them on faith. In this way, the Gospels and other ancient writings about Jesus remain fascinating to both believers and non-believers.

Childhood and Young Adulthood

The Bible says Jesus's mother was named Mary, and according to the Gospel of Luke, God sent the angel Gabriel to tell the unmarried Mary that she had found favor with God and would miraculously conceive a son, through the power of the Holy Spirit of God. The angel told the same to Joseph, Mary's future husband and the man who would raise Jesus.

The Gospels say that Mary and Joseph were traveling through Judea to be counted in the latest Roman census, when Mary went into labor. The birth of Jesus took place in the small village of Bethlehem, located about eighty miles south of their hometown of Nazareth, in northern Palestine. The story of the birth of Jesus is called the Nativity.

The exact year of Jesus's birth is uncertain. The vast majority of scholars accept 4 BCE, give or take a year or two. It used to be assumed that the correct year was CE 1 because the widely used Christian calendar begins with that date. The problem is that the calendar in question was introduced more than five centuries after Jesus died. By that time, no one could remember his actual dates. So the monk who created the calendar, Dionysius

An angel telling shepherds in Bethlehem of the birth of Jesus Christ in an 1872 print.

Exiguus, estimated as best as he could. Modern experts determined that he was off by about four years, which, given what he had to work with, was extremely good work.

After Mary, Joseph, and Jesus returned to Nazareth, the boy began his upbringing, about which extremely little is known. When his parents deemed him old enough, Jesus may have learned Joseph's trade. Most ancient sources suggest that they

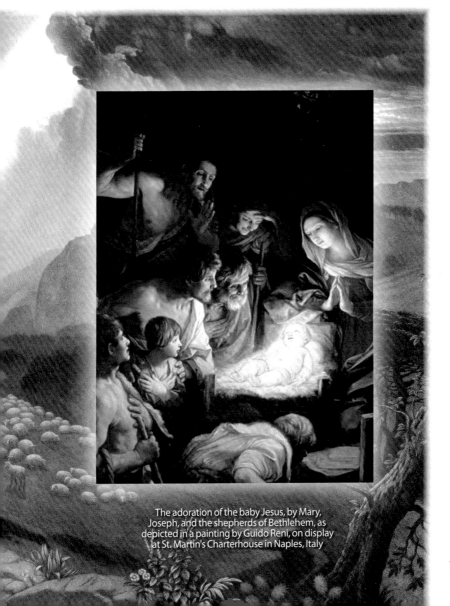

The adoration of the baby Jesus, by Mary, Joseph, and the shepherds of Bethlehem, as depicted in a painting by Guido Reni, on display at St. Martin's Charterhouse in Naples, Italy

were carpenters, although some scholars have suggested they were stonemasons. Either Mary or Joseph, or both, seemed to have taught the boy about the Hebrew scriptures. He certainly knew a great deal about them by age twelve, as related in one of the episodes in the Gospels. It tells how the family journeyed to Judea's capital, Jerusalem, for the important Jewish holiday called Passover. When the festival ended and Mary and Joseph were ready to depart, they could not find Jesus. Three days later they located him in the city's great temple. He was sitting with some Jewish scholars, conversing and asking them questions. These men were amazed at how well Jesus knew the scriptures.

From his twelfth year to his late twenties, nothing for sure is known about what Jesus did and said. Some people assume that he continued to work with Joseph until the latter died, sometime in Jesus's teens or twenties. Other people have speculated that Jesus lived and/or studied with the Essenes. Members of a Jewish sect, they were monk-like hermits who dwelled in the desert wilderness near the Dead Sea, and they are thought to have produced the Dead Sea Scrolls. The Essenes preached that the end-days were near. Soon, they claimed, the Messiah would come and then a violent upheaval would transform the world, ushering in the Kingdom of God.

Some scholars feel there is reason to believe that Jesus's cousin, John the Baptist, was an Essene. But to date, no one has uncovered any solid proof that Jesus also belonged to that group.

The Baptist

Wherever and however Jesus spent those undocumented years, the first major recorded event of his adulthood was his baptism by his cousin. John, an outspoken, controversial preacher, had been earning his nickname, the Baptist, by baptizing Jews in the

Jordan River. He frequently warned that the Messiah and God's Kingdom were at hand and called on people to repent their sins before it was too late. Because he had such a forthright, magnetic personality, some people believed he was the very Messiah he spoke of. But John corrected them. He said that the real Messiah was still to come and would be so great that he, John, was not worthy even to carry his sandals. According to the Gospels, as Jesus drew near the Jordan River John suddenly realized that his cousin was the Messiah. Jesus calmly stepped into the water and waited to be baptized. But John insisted that it was Jesus that should baptize *him* and not the other way around. In response, Jesus supposedly said, "Let it be so now. [It] is fitting for us to fulfill all righteousness." Then John baptized Jesus.

It was not long after Jesus's baptism that John got into some serious trouble. The Baptist publicly scolded Herod Antipas, the Jewish leader then ruling Galilee (part of Judea) for the Romans. The disreputable deed John singled out was Herod's recent marriage to his own brother's wife. The angry Herod at first imprisoned John and then had him executed.

Jesus's Ministry

The Baptist was no longer around to promote the idea of the fast approaching Kingdom of God. But Jesus was. He started a ministry of his own, choosing twelve close followers called apostles. They came from various social groups, but most were poor and uneducated. Also among his followers were two women, Mary Magdalene and Mary of Bethany. The latter was the sister of Jesus's good friend Lazarus.

Mary Magdalene's exact identity is unclear. For many centuries a majority of Christians, including scholars, thought she was a prostitute or some other kind of sinner whom Jesus

The Baptism of Christ, an 1873 print

had befriended. But in recent years most experts have discounted that theory. She is now seen as an old and close friend of Jesus's in her own right. It is possible they met in his youth and remained together after he began preaching. In any case, some of the Jewish and Christian writings that did not make it into the Bible call her the "apostle to the apostle." This suggests that she was more important to Jesus than the other apostles, although the precise nature of their relationship remains a mystery. (Some researchers have hypothesized that she was Jesus's wife; but most biblical scholars say there is no compelling evidence for this contention.) Whoever Mary was and whatever her role in Jesus's life and ministry may have been, it appears she stayed at his side always.

The four biblical Gospels claim that among the many incidents Mary and Jesus's other followers witnessed were several miracles. It was said that he could heal such ailments as paralysis, blindness, possession by demons, and leprosy. The latter, which was fairly common in ancient societies, was a disease that caused bodily disfiguration. Healthy people often forced lepers to live on their own in small, isolated small colonies. The Gospels say that one day while Jesus was teaching, a leper came to him and asked to be healed. Jesus proceeded to touch the man and the leprosy quickly disappeared.

According to the Gospels, some people who witnessed this and other miracles that Jesus performed were amazed. They saw him as a great healer, someone blessed by God. As a result, his reputation grew and he drew large crowds almost everywhere he went.

At times Jesus lectured hundreds of people at a time, though the exact numbers were never recorded. Some people who came to hear him speak tried to touch his robe, hoping the force of his spirit would give them greater strength and faith. Others were happy just to sit back and listen to what he had to say.

In addition to reminding people that God's Kingdom was imminent, Jesus urged people to be as ethical and honest as possible. He also vigorously promoted the concepts of love, brotherhood, and peace. In addition, he called for decent treatment of people who were poor and oppressed. In later ages, his most famous single speech came to be called the Sermon on the Mount. (No one knows for sure where it took place.) In the speech, he touched on almost all the principal elements of his outlook on life, including peace, mercy, love, and forgiveness. Among the numerous memorable passages from the speech, which appears in the Gospel of Matthew, are the following:

Blessed are the poor in spirit, for theirs is the kingdom of heaven. Blessed are those who mourn, for they shall be comforted. Blessed are the meek, for they shall inherit the earth. Blessed are those who hunger and thirst for righteousness, for they shall be satisfied. Blessed are the merciful, for they shall obtain mercy. Blessed are the pure in heart, for they shall see God. Blessed are the peacemakers, for they shall be called sons of God. Blessed are those who are persecuted for righteousness' sake, for theirs is the kingdom of heaven.

Death in Jerusalem

Jesus continued his ministry for an unknown number of months or years. Eventually he decided to go to Jerusalem during the next Passover celebration. By this time his name was well known throughout Judea, and as he entered the city large numbers of people crowded the streets hoping to get a look at him. He came riding on a donkey and soon went to the great temple.

There, in the structure's courtyard, the Gospels say, Jesus beheld several money changers plying their trade. During the Passover festival, custom dictated that only Jewish money could be used. So these men exchanged standard Greek and Roman coins for Jewish ones. Jesus was outraged by this spectacle because he felt that business dealings defiled the temple grounds; he said they should be used only for prayer. So he overthrew the tables of the money changers, causing a huge commotion.

This bold act, which was witnessed by many bystanders, upset the temple priests as well as the Jewish authorities. It is impossible to know what these men were thinking. But some evidence suggests that they already felt threatened by Jesus because of his power to sway large crowds. Also, he may have more than once spoken out against them, questioning their authority in some way. For these reasons, and perhaps for others lost to history, they saw him as a troublemaker and decided to punish or kill him.

The rest of Jesus's well-known story, as told in the Gospels, has been reenacted and dramatized countless times in paintings, novels, stage plays, and movies. To celebrate Passover, he and the apostles had a meal, which became known as the "Last Supper." During the meal, Jesus took a piece of bread and blessed and broke it, saying, "Take, eat: this is my body." Then he took a cup of wine and blessed it saying, "Drink of it, all of you, for this is my blood . . . which is poured out for many for the forgiveness of sins." (An unknown number of years later, Christians used this incident as the basis for the ritual of the Eucharist, or Holy Communion.)

After the supper, one of these twelve followers, Judas, betrayed Jesus. Judas took money from the authorities in exchange for pointing him out to the arresting soldiers. Jesus was indeed arrested, and according to the Gospel of Matthew all the disciples fled. The next day Jesus was tried and found guilty of blasphemy (showing disrespect for sacred beliefs or customs). Although the Sanhedrin could try and convict someone, the Romans did not allow it to carry out a death sentence.

Top: Jacopo Bassano's *The Last Supper*, a 1546 oil painting of Jesus (standing in the center) with his disciples at the moment he asks who among them will betray him. The painting is on display at the Galleria Borghese in Rome, Italy.

Bottom: *Cristo crucifado* by Diego Velázquez, a 1632 oil painting depicting the body of Jesus nailed to a wooden cross, on display at the Museo del Prado in Madrid, Spain

Only the Roman authorities could do that. So the Sanhedrin handed Jesus over to the Roman governor, Pontius Pilate, who ordered him to be executed by crucifixion, then a common form of capital punishment.

The execution was said to have taken place on a hill outside the city. Mary Magdalene, along with Jesus's mother Mary, took charge of the body after it was over. The Gospels say that a man named Joseph, who owned a tomb nearby, helped them. They placed Jesus's remains in the tomb and sealed it with a heavy stone.

Later, the Gospels continue, Mary Magdalene visited the tomb and found that the stone had been moved away. Jesus's body had disappeared and she and the apostles became convinced that their dead master had come back to life. This became known as the Resurrection. It would prove to be a key element in the efforts to keep the memory of Jesus and his teaching alive after his passing.

Judgment Day Imminent?

In the months directly after Jesus died, his followers were relatively few in number. Some may have felt that Jesus might be the predicted Messiah while he was still alive. This is supported by a passage in the Gospel of Matthew, in which Jesus's apostle Peter tells him, "You are the Christ, the son of the living God." The title "Christ" was another name for Messiah. As the passage goes on, Jesus appears to confirm what Peter said and asks the apostles not to tell anyone that he, Jesus, is the Christ. (Peter, one of Jesus's closest apostles, is generally considered by Roman Catholics to be the first pope.)

Devout Christians see the passage as proof not only that the apostles thought Jesus might be the Messiah, but also that he himself *knew* he was. However, many scholars think this exchange between Jesus and Peter never happened. They suggest that whoever wrote Matthew several decades later added it in order to strengthen the contention that Jesus was the Messiah.

Even if the apostles had not been certain that Jesus was the Messiah while he was living, they enthusiastically promoted that idea after his death. Devout Christians say this was partly because the resurrected Jesus appeared to them not long after the crucifixion. According to the Gospel of Luke, he told them:

It is written, that the Christ should suffer and on the third day rise from the dead, and that repentance and forgiveness of sins should be preached in his name to all nations, beginning from Jerusalem. You are witnesses of these things. And behold, I send the promise of my Father [God] upon you.

A number of biblical scholars and other experts think that this exchange, too, was likely added later. They point out that Jesus's immediate followers may have sincerely believed he had been resurrected from the dead. And that may have been enough to convince them that he was Messiah.

Whatever their reasons, the apostles seem to have been sure that they would meet Jesus again in their own lifetimes. This was because they strongly believed what he had fervently preached— that the Messiah would be arriving on Earth in the very near future. So in their view it was more important than ever to spread the word about the imminent coming of Judgment Day.

The targets of their preaching, just as Jesus's had been, were other Jews. They had no reason to reach out to non-Jews, or Gentiles.

After all, they likely reasoned, the Jewish god was going to smite the Romans and many other Gentiles who had long oppressed the Jews. And with the establishment of God's Kingdom, the Jews, the "chosen people," would stand in humanity's forefront.

Paul's Momentous Revelations

As Jesus's followers began to spread the "good news" of his imminent return, his followers organized themselves into a group, calling themselves the people of "the Way." (The term Christian had not yet been coined.) Though they were quite earnest, they found that finding new converts to their cause was daunting. The majority of other Jews did not believe them when they said Jesus was the Messiah and would be arriving in the near future. Many Jews became suspicious of or annoyed by the group. It did not help when one of its members, Stephen, loudly announced that Jerusalem's great temple would soon be demolished in the turmoil of Judgment Day. Seeing Stephen as another radical troublemaker, the authorities had him executed. Soon the members of the Way found themselves being persecuted by fellow Jews.

It was at this point, with Jesus's followers in increasingly dire straits, that Paul came on the scene. His original name was Saul of Tarsus. And he was among those who vigorously persecuted the Way. In fact, he decided to go to Damascus (in Syria, just north of Palestine) to capture some of Jesus's followers who had fled there. But during the trip, according to the Gospels, he suddenly had a momentous revelation. The biblical Book of Acts reports his saying:

About noon a great light from heaven suddenly shone about me. And I fell to the ground and heard a voice saying to me, 'Saul, Saul, why do you persecute me?' And I answered, 'Who are you, Lord?' And he said to me, 'I am Jesus of Nazareth whom you are persecuting.'

In a remarkable reversal, Paul soon became one of the most ardent members of the Way. Like the others, he worried the group might fade away if new converts could not be found. Some members of the group had already approached Gentiles. But the latter were expected to become Jews when they joined, and that included adopting Jewish customs. These included strict dietary laws and practicing circumcision. Most Gentiles saw circumcision as repulsive and refused to join. And this led Paul to another momentous revelation. He persuaded the group's leaders to drop the requirement that new recruits had to become Jews.

A New Faith

In inviting non-Jews into what might be called the Jesus movement, Paul was not trying to start a new religion. He was a Jew, as were the apostles, and they worshiped the Jewish God. They also revered the Jewish scriptures (the Old Testament) and followed Jewish rituals and customs. Like other members of the Way, Paul was convinced that God's Kingdom would come in the very near future. He thought it would be humane and ethical to teach both Jews and Gentiles about the new world that would soon come to pass.

However, what actually came to pass could not have been foreseen. The Kingdom of God did not arrive in their lifetimes, nor in the centuries that immediately followed. Instead, more and more Gentiles became followers of Jesus and his teachings. At the same time, these non-Jewish followers broke away from the Jewish ones, in the process creating a new faith: Christianity.

Opposite Page: *The Conversion of Saint Paul* by Federico and Taddeo Zuccari. The 1563 painting, on display at San Marcello al Corso, a church in Rome, Italy, shows Jesus appearing to Paul (bottom, center).

The name "Muhammad" in traditional Thuluth calligraphy (a form of
Islamic calligraphy) by Hattat Aziz Efendi, an Ottoman calligrapher

Chapter

7

Muhammad

Muhammad (or Mohammed) was, and remains, the pivotal prophet of the religion known as Islam. Muslims, as those who follow Islam are called, believe that a long line of prophets preceded Muhammad. They included Adam, Noah, Abraham, Moses, and Jesus, among others.

It is no coincidence that these are also major figures in the Jewish and Christian scriptures, the books that make up the Bible. Muhammad and the faith he founded were strongly influenced by those other two monotheistic faiths. Indeed, Muslims believe that Allah and the deity worshiped by Christians and Jews are one and the same. Further, the followers of Islam hold, the three faiths are in a sense sister religions. Muslims collectively call themselves, Jews, and Christians *ahl al-kitab,* or the "People of the Book." By the "book," they mean the sacred writings of these religions. For Jews the book is the Torah. For Christians it is the Old and New Testament. And for Muslims it is the Qur'an (or Koran).

The three faiths are also sometimes called the "Abrahamic" religions. This is because each sees the biblical character Abraham as a major early prophet or father-figure. Muslims believe that Abraham journeyed to Arabia. There, they say, he constructed the holy shrine called the Kaaba (or Kaba), a large cube-shaped structure, in what would later become the sacred city of Mecca. Muslims also believe that a large proportion of Arabs are descended from Abraham's son Ishmael.

Although Muslims revere Abraham, Jesus, and other earlier leading religious figures, they view Muhammad as the last and most important of the prophets. Supposedly, like many other Arabs, he was descended directly from Abraham. Moreover, Muslims believe that God chose Muhammad to receive a revelation, consisting of the words of the holy Qur'an. According to the basic tenets of Islam, God also instructed Muhammad to go out and preach the principles outlined in the Qur'an.

Multi-ethnic Mecca

Muhammad's story begins in Mecca, situated in western Arabia near the coast of the Red Sea. Historians have determined that before Islam arose in the area, Mecca was an important trading center. Its merchants traveled as far away as Syria in the north, Egypt in the northwest, and Ethiopia in the west, as well as to southern Arabia. And traders from those and other foreign lands sometimes brought caravans filled with goods to Mecca.

Krasnodar

Gora El'brus
18,510 ft

Sochi

CAUCASUS

ack Sea

Stavropol

Groznyy

Vladikavkaz

Aqtau

UZE

GEORGIA

Tbilisi

Samsun

ARM.

Yerevan

Baku

Ganca

AZERBAIJAN

Turkmenbasy

TURKME

Ankara

R K E Y

Mt. Ararat
16,854 ft

Tabriz

Lake
Urmia

Rasht

Tehran

Mashha

ana

Gaziantep

Halab

Mosul

Hamadan

Qom

Esfahan

I R A N

Hims

SYRIA

Euphrates

Baghdad

Dezful

Yazd

Kern

LEB.

eirut

Damascus

IRAQ

Ar Rutbah

Tigris

Abadan

AEL

fo

Amman

An Najaf

Al Basrah

KUW.

Shiraz

Jerusalem

JOR.

Al Jawf

Al Kuwayt

ez

Mt. Katrina
8668 ft

SAUDI

Al Manamah

BAHRAIN

QATAR

Persian

Banda

g

ARABIA

Ad Dawhah

Dubayy

Abu Dhabi

Aswan

Medina

Riyadh

Gulf

U.A.E.

Arabian
Peninsula

Red Sea

Jiddah

Mecca

OMAN

ort Sudan

Rub Al-Khali

hartoum

Wad Madani

ERITREA

Asmara

Sanaa

YEMEN

Mirbat

Al Hudaydah

Al Mukalla

Ras Deien

den

As a result, the town became large, prosperous, and both multi-ethnic and multi-religious. By the early sixth century CE its residents included not only Arabs, but also Jews, Persians (many of whom revered the ancient Persian prophet Zoroaster), and Christians. Also residing there were people whose parents or grandparents had originated in many different parts of the Middle East.

In addition, Mecca was one of the main, if not *the* main, religious center in the Arabian Peninsula. At the time, the Arabs were polytheistic, which meant that they worshiped many gods. Members of various Arabian tribes, each with its own god or gods, periodically made a religious pilgrimage to Mecca. This trip was called a hajj. The object of the journey was to take part in special rituals.

Among these rituals was a visit to the Kaaba, which Abraham was said to have erected many centuries before. More than three hundred statues of tribal gods had been set up inside the Kaaba. It was therefore seen as an extremely holy place, so holy that those tribes that were at war at the time of a hajj temporarily laid down their arms while worshiping in Mecca. Muslims believe that one reason why God singled out Muhammad was to put an end to this polytheistic idol-worship and to turn all hearts toward Allah, the one true God.

Muhammad's Childhood

According to Islamic tradition, Muhammad was born in Mecca in the year 570. He was a member of the Hashim clan. In Arab society a few families made up a clan, and several clans made up a tribe. Muhammad's tribe was the Quraysh, whose members were mostly traders as well as among Mecca's leading citizens.

Muhammad never met his father, who had died before he was born. His mother, Amina, did her best to raise the child by herself. But she found it too difficult and soon searched for a family that would care for him until she was up to the task. She eventually found a shepherd family that dwelled in a mountain valley not far from Mecca. It was said that the young boy did well in his new home and enjoyed playing with his foster brothers.

Later, perhaps when Muhammad was five, Amina was able to bring him to live with her in Mecca. However, she passed away when he was six, leaving him an orphan. Fortunately for the grief-stricken boy, his father's father, Abdul Muttalib, gladly took him in with the intention of raising him like his own son. Apparently very attentive to Muhammad, Muttalib told him stories about the adventures of traders and merchants traveling across the desert in camel caravans.

In 578, when Muhammad was eight, his grandfather died, and this time his uncle, Abu Talib, took him in. According to tradition, in the years that followed the young man never learned to read or to write. Yet he had a fertile imagination and spent much time meditating and thinking about why the world and society were the way they were.

Another story claims that when Muhammad was twelve his uncle took him along on a trading trip to Syria. On the way, a Christian monk invited the caravan to stop and eat. The merchants had traveled this route many times, and the holy man had never before invited them to stop. Unknown to them, the monk had seen a cloud shade the caravan from the heat of the sun. And when the caravan stopped to rest near the oasis, a tree lowered its branches to shade Muhammad.

The merchants accepted the old monk's invitation. While they ate, the monk noticed a mark between Muhammad's shoulders that supposedly appeared only on the bodies of prophets. So the monk questioned the boy, especially about his dreams. Muhammad's answers convinced the monk that there was indeed something special about him. The holy man took Abu Talib aside and advised him to return to his home country with his nephew and guard him, for some people might seek to do the boy harm.

Talib heeded this advice and returned with Muhammad to Mecca. There, the young man spent long hours at the Kaaba, the town's leading shrine. He carefully watched the religious rituals of the various tribesmen. Although Muhammad's family worshiped some of the gods that had statues in the Kaaba, he had been learning about the beliefs of the Jews and Christians who lived in Mecca. And over time he developed doubts about the traditional Arab gods. The single deity worshiped by the Jews and Christians appealed more to him. At least this is how the surviving accounts of his life tell it. Modern scholars point out that there is no way to know for sure if the young man gave much thought to religion until he was older.

Work and Marriage

Eventually, Muhammad became old enough to engage in a trade. Exactly what it was is uncertain. But most of the available evidence suggests that he joined the same business that most of his relatives and friends were in—merchandizing. It is likely that

A panorama of Al-Masjid al-Haram, the Sacred Mosque, in Mecca, Saudi Arabia he went on caravans to neighboring lands. He might also have worked sometimes in Mecca, maybe buying and selling various goods in local markets.

When the young man was twenty-five, a well-to-do woman named Khadija hired him to conduct a caravan to Syria. Legend claims that as the caravan was returning, Khadija, who was standing at a distance, saw two angels hovering over Muhammad, seemingly protecting him from the sun. Whether or not this actually occurred, more certain is that Khadija was impressed by the way Muhammad had handled the caravan. She also came to admire his sense of responsibility and humility, and after a few months she offered him her hand in marriage. She likely felt comfortable making this offer because first, she was fifteen years older than he was, and second, she was financially better-off than he was.

Their marriage made Muhammad a rich man. He showed no interest in her money, however. Instead, he enjoyed her company because he loved and respected her above all other women. In fact, although at the time it was permitted in Arab society for a man to have more than one wife, he took no others as long as Khadija lived.

As time went on, Muhammad spent less and less time accompanying the caravans. He came to spend much of his free time in the hills, where he sought solitude so he could meditate, think, and pray. Sometimes he was away from town and his wife for

weeks at a time. (He was not the only person to do this. Meccan men who periodically went out into the countryside to be alone and think about religion and the meaning of life were called *hanif*.) On one of these outings, in the year 610, Muhammad found a cave on the slopes of Jabal an-Nur, a mountain not far from Mecca. In that cave, which came to be called the Cave of Hira, he had an experience that was destined to change both his own life and eventually the world.

A Frightening Visitor

The often-told story goes that Muhammad fell asleep in the cave and after a while awoke to the sound of a loud voice. It turned out to belong to the angel Gabriel, who had taken human form in order to communicate with Muhammad. The angel commanded the man to begin reciting. But Muhammad, who was frightened by the sudden appearance of this strange apparition, did not know what he was supposed to recite. And besides, he was illiterate. "I am not [one] of those who read," he told the angel. Hearing this, Gabriel walked over to the man and held him so tightly that he could hardly breathe. Then he again ordered Muhammad to recite. Muhammad, who was now even more frightened, repeated, "I am not [one] of those who read." Once more the angel grabbed hold of him and this time squeezed so tightly he almost choked. Again the superhuman being demanded that Muhammad recite.

Eventually Muhammad, who had never before read from a book, started to read and recite words written on a piece of cloth the angel held before him. The words he spoke turned out to be the first lines of the Qur'an:

Recite in the name of your Lord who created:
He created man from a clot of blood.
Recite: and your Lord is the most Bountiful
He who has taught by the pen,
Taught man what he knew not.

A twelfth-century icon of the Angel Gabriel

The traditional account goes on to tell how Muhammad, having recited words he had never even heard before, sank to the ground in a state of terror. At first he wondered if he had been possessed by an evil spirit. Covering his face, he felt his body tremble. His forehead broke out in beads of perspiration. He was so fearful, in fact, that he considered climbing to the top of the mountain and jumping off to his death.

But before the man could do away with himself, he had another vision of the angel. "When I was midway on [my climb up] the mountain," Muhammad later recalled, "I heard a voice from heaven saying: 'O Muhammad! You are the apostle of God and I am Gabriel.' I raised my head towards heaven to see who was speaking, and lo, [there was] Gabriel in the form of a man with feet [standing] astride the horizon."

After the vision, Muhammad rushed home to his wife and told her what had happened. Her immediate reaction is unknown. But various legendary accounts say that Khadija suspected at once that her husband had experienced a supernatural vision. She agreed with the angel that Muhammad might indeed be a prophet of Allah. If so, she pointed out, God would guide him. Because she believed her husband, she became the first convert to what would eventually be a new religion—Islam.

Khadija wasted no time in telling Muhammad's cousin, Ali ibn Abi Talib, what had occurred. Ali knew a fair amount about the beliefs and backgrounds of Judaism and Christianity. He informed her that the angel who appeared to her husband might well be the same one that the Bible said God sent to Moses. In addition, Ali recalled that the same angel was said to have visited Jesus's parents. If this was the case, Ali declared, then Mohammad must be a prophet of God, as he claimed he was. Accordingly, Ali became Muhammad's second convert.

A painting of Ali ibn Abi Talib, Muhammad's cousin, by Ahmad Reza Haraji. Ali was appointed caliph, or the spiritual leader of Islam succeeding Muhammad, and reigned from 656 CE to 661 CE.

For awhile, Muhammad confided his revelations only to his closest relatives. He always insisted that he was not himself divine, but merely a man chosen to be the spokesman of Allah. Meanwhile, the divine revelations from Gabriel continued. And on each occasion Muhammad recited more verses of the growing Qur'an.

Muhammad Begins Preaching

One of the first people, after Ali and Khadija, to become a believer was Muhammad's young servant, Zayd. Years before, a band of thieves had sold the youth to Muhammad, and after a while the boy's father had found out that his son was in Mecca. He had offered Muhammad a large sum of money for the boy. But Muhammad told Zayd's father that if the boy wished to go with him, he could go without a ransom or other payment. On the other hand, if Zayd chose to stay with Muhammad and Khadija, he would be welcome to do so.

Zayd thought it over and then told his father that Muhammad and Khadija had treated him more as a son than as a slave. So he wished to stay with them. Zayd's father accepted this, and Muhammad was so pleased that he officially adopted the boy. Partly because of these kindnesses, Zayd remained devoted to Muhammad throughout his life.

In the meantime, the recitations Muhammad kept receiving from the angel began to form a coherent religious message, or philosophy of life and the relationship between humans and God. This philosophy was similar in some ways to those of the other monotheistic faiths that had emerged in the Middle East. One modern author and scholar sums it up concisely, saying:

The message was similar to those received by the early Hebrew prophets: that God is one, he is all-powerful, he is the creator of the universe, and that there will be a Judgment Day when those who have carried out God's commands will enjoy paradise in heaven, and those who have not will be condemned to hell. . . . These ideas were also part of the Zoroastrian religion [practiced in Persia].

At first, Muhammad preached these basic concepts only to a small group of people in Mecca. But after more time had passed, the angel Gabriel ordered him to preach the new faith to people beyond his hometown. Even then, Muhammad likely did not foresee that said faith would become a major new religion and gain converts well beyond the lands of the Middle East.

After he had been commanded to begin preaching, Muhammad walked through Mecca, telling the people about the new religious ideas he had learned. His duty, he said, was to show people the importance of worshiping Allah, the one true God. Unlike the statue of a deity, Muhammad said, Allah, who had created the world and humanity, was invisible.

But most people who heard Muhammad preach were uncomfortable about the idea of worshiping an invisible god. Those who had known Muhammad from childhood, or who remembered him as a hard-working merchant, thought he must be losing his mind. They questioned his claim that God had appointed him the last of a long line of prophets. Soon they were sneering at him as he walked through the streets. They called him a crazy man who thought he knew what was going on in heaven, something that human beings should have no way of knowing. Muhammad became so widely disliked that people started shouting him down when he tried to speak. Some threw dirt on him as he prayed. Also, when they challenged him to perform miracles, he quoted the Qur'an, saying: "I am but a messenger!" Hearing this, the onlookers called him a fake.

Death Threats and the Hegira

Matters became even worse when Muhammad denounced the gods whose statues adorned the Kaaba. They were mere idols, he said, while Allah was the real God. Hearing this attack on traditional beliefs, Mecca's leading citizens began seeing Muhammad not just as a local lunatic, but also as a threat to society. They worried that such radical ideas would insult many of the tribesmen who journeyed to Mecca each year. These visitors spent a great deal of money while they were in the city. And much of that money might be lost if Muhammad's ravings kept people from going on the hajj.

Another way Muhammad posed a threat was the way in which he challenged society's existing power structure. He claimed to be a religious authority. In Arabian society men holding public authority were viewed as being smarter and more worthy of obedience than others. If people started accepting Muhammad's religion, they might begin seeing him as their political leader as well. And that would be bad for the existing leaders.

Fortunately for Muhammad, he was under the protection of his uncle's tribe. So at first the town elders could not get rid of or punish Muhammad. However, as time went on, more and more people came to believe that Muhammad was indeed a person blessed by God and not the madman the authorities claimed he was.

One reason Muhammad won over so many people was that he lived his faith and did so in deep humility. Whenever he met a poor man, he invited him home to share his meal of bread, figs, or dates. Also, any slave could come to him and demand justice. If the slave devoted himself to Islam, he immediately became a free man. In addition, Muhammad listened when people needed to talk and happily taught those who needed teaching. Finally, he continued to preach the word of the one true God. And he never claimed to be anything beyond a mere man.

Because of Muhammad's rising popularity, his enemies began to plot against him. Making matters worse for him, in 619, when he was around fifty, his wife and uncle both died. Not only did Muhammad have to struggle with his grief at losing Khadija, he also had to face the fact that he could no longer count on the tribal protection he had long enjoyed.

In the months that followed, it became increasingly clear that Muhammad's life was in imminent danger. Moreover, his few dozen converts to Islam were also at risk of being hunted down and killed for their so-called dangerous beliefs. At this point Muhammad remembered that some men from the town of Yathrib, located about 215 miles north of Mecca, had recently paid him a visit. They had urged Muhammad to move, along with his followers, to their town. There, they would be given protection.

Muhammad decided it would be wise to accept this offer. He secretly sent most of his followers to Yathrib, which soon afterward became known as Medina. But before Muhammad himself could leave for Medina, the Meccan elders found out what was happening. They ordered a group of men to assassinate the Muslim leader. On July 16, 622, just as the killers were closing on them, Muhammad and his good friend Abu Bakr escaped. They hurried toward Medina, realizing that the assassins were in pursuit.

After managing to elude the pursuers for three days, the two men made it to Medina, where they were welcomed with open arms. From that day forward, Muslims called the flight from Mecca to Medina the Hegira, meaning "emigration." And, as a result, 622 became a major turning point in Islamic history. It was, and still is, seen as the true beginning of the Muslims' faith. For that reason, it marks the first year of the Islamic calendar.

Winning Over Mecca

The move to Medina was also a major turning point for Muhammad. No longer was he an often ridiculed preacher doing his best to spread the word of Islam in the city streets. Almost overnight he became a major statesman and politician, as well as a prophet and teacher who was widely respected in his new home.

Muhammad bought a plot of land in that home city. He also erected a mosque, a church-like building where Muslims could pray and discuss Islam and its beliefs. Muhammad also laid out certain strict rules that members of the new faith were expected to follow. According to the Qur'an, he said, the faithful had to avoid gambling, drinking alcohol, lying, and stealing. That sacred book also taught that Muslims must not be the aggressors in war.

The painting *Ansicht von Mekka in Arabien* by Hubert Sattler depicts a view of Mecca and the Kaaba circa 1897. The painting is on display at the Salzburg Museum in Salzburg, Austria.

However, if an injustice had been done, they should not hesitate to fight until the enemy surrendered.

Each person who joined the faith was also expected to make ties to tribe and family secondary to devotion to Islam. This was only fitting, Muhammad explained, since the term Islam meant complete submission to God. But one major threat to the success of the new religion was that the leading Meccans still opposed it and its founder. Violent conflict between Mecca and Medina was brewing. And Muhammad decided that his best strategy was to deal with the problem head-on. As University of Calgary scholar Erica Fraser tells it:

> In 624, Mohammed decided the Medinans should intercept a camel caravan on its way from Syria to Mecca, for the purpose of disrupting Meccan economic activity and obtaining the cargo for his followers. In the resulting Battle of Badr, the Medinans won a decisive victory despite being outnumbered by the Meccans. The event served to unify the Medinans and weaken the Meccans. It was also the first significant victory in battle for a people who would soon grow into [a] formidable military force. [The victory also] strengthened Mohammed's resolve to bring Mecca under Muslim control, and several more battles were fought between the two cities.

Mecca was progressively weakened by the continued Muslim tactic of interrupting caravan traffic, and by 630, the city fell to the Muslims with little resistance.

After gaining control of Mecca, Muhammad demonstrated that he was at heart a man of peace, not war. He instituted a general amnesty, making it known that none of the town's residents would be punished for their former hostility toward him and his followers. Thankful, many Meccans now gave Islam serious consideration. And the faith began taking hold in the town. When he felt the time was right, Muhammad took the bold step of removing the statues of the traditional Arab gods from the Kaaba. That monument now became a holy shrine and spiritual center for all Muslims.

The Fastest Growing Religion

Mecca was not the only town the Muslims won over to their side. With Muhammad leading them, they conducted campaigns throughout the Arabian Peninsula, until nearly all Arabs were united under Islam's banners. Soon, idol worship became a practice of the past.

At age sixty-three, Muhammad's work was nearly over. He took one final pilgrimage from Medina to his boyhood city of Mecca, where he preached his last sermon and received his final revelation from the angel Gabriel. Then he returned to Medina.

Hoping to give a parting sermon in Medina, Muhammad made his way to the mosque he had built. He told his gathered followers that everything happens according to Allah's will and at a time appointed by the one and only true God. He added it was now time for Muhammad himself to leave and meet Allah in heaven. Then he said:

O people, listen to me closely. Serve God, say your five daily prayers, fast during the month of Ramadan, and give of your wealth [to] charity. [O] people, no prophet will come after me, and no new way of life will be born. [Therefore] be my witness, O God, that I have conveyed Your Message to Your people.

Muhammad then walked slowly to his house and laid down. Raising his eyes toward heaven, he murmured, "My Lord, help me bear the pangs of death." According to some medieval accounts, those were his last words.

Though he himself was gone, Muhammad left behind an enormous legacy. While he was living, the faith he had founded had spread across all of Arabia in only a few years. After his death, it was destined to reach a great deal farther with almost lightning speed. Less than a century after his passing, Muslims were in control of Syria, Iraq, Persia, Palestine, Egypt, and large sections of North Africa.

That proved to be only the beginning. Today Islam has more than a billion followers and is the fastest growing major religion. The Qur'an consists of several thousand verses arranged in 114 chapters. Passages and phrases from it are memorized and recited in classical Arabic by Muslims every day. And, Muslims across the world still revere their long line of prophets, including the man they see as the last in that distinguished group. Following the rituals that Muhammad himself established, each and every day the faithful repeat the phrase: "There is no god but God, and Muhammad is his messenger."

Timeline

BCE	ca. 3228	Krishna is born.
	ca. 3213	Krishna moves to Vrindaban and according to legend kills a demon.
	ca. 3212-3196	Krishna lives in Mathura and advises the national rulers.
	ca. 3103	Krishna dies at age 125.
	ca. 1995	Abraham is born.
	ca. 1920	God commands Abraham to leave his father's household and go to an unknown land.
	ca. 1918	Migrates to Egypt to avoid a famine in Canaan.
	ca. 1911	God appears to Abraham and makes a formal covenant with him.
	ca. 1909	Birth of Abraham's first son, Ishmael, whose mother is Hagar, Sarah's Egyptian maid.
	ca. 1896	God confirms his covenant with Abraham.
	ca. 1895	Second son, Isaac, is born.
	ca. 1882	God commands Abraham to sacrifice Isaac; Abraham obeys and God spares the child at the last moment and substitutes a ram.
	ca. 1858	Sarah dies.
	ca. 1855	Abraham takes another wife, Keturah, who bears him six sons.
	ca. 1820	Dies at the age of 175.
	ca. 628	Zoroaster is born in a town near the Caspian Sea, in ancient Persia.
	ca. 608-598	He leaves home to seek the truth about good and evil.
	ca. 598	At age thirty, Zoroaster experiences illumination.
	ca. 586	He converts King Vishtaspa and is appointed high priest in the royal palace.
	ca. 586-584	Zoroaster languishes in prison.

BCE	ca. 584	He is reinstalled as high priest; his disciples begin to spread the message of his holy book, the *Avesta*.
	ca. 563	Siddhartha Gautama is born in Lumbini, India, near modern day Nepal.
	ca. 551	Zoroaster is killed while praying in a temple; Confucius is born in China.
	ca. 547	At age sixteen Siddhartha marries a young woman named Yasodhara.
	ca. 533	Siddhartha sees an old man, a sick man, a dead man, and a holy monk.
	ca. 534	At age twenty-nine, Siddhartha gives up life as a prince and begins seeking enlightenment; Confucius works as a supervisor of grain storage.
	ca. 531	Confucius's son, Li, is born.
	ca. 526	Siddhartha attains enlightenment and thereby becomes the Buddha.
	ca. 525	Confucius begins teaching.
	ca. 523-483	Buddha teaches large numbers of people across India.
	ca. 519	War breaks out in the Chinese state of Lu.
	ca. 518	Confucius leaves home to travel and meets the Taoist sage Lao-Tzu.
	ca. 518-500	Confucius attempts to persuade various rulers to follow his philosophy.
	ca. 501	He becomes chief magistrate of the city of Chung-tu.
	ca. 498	He is appointed to the post of prime minister of Lu.
	ca. 483	Buddha dies in a forest near Kusinara, Nepal, at age eighty.
	ca. 482	Confucius writes a history of Lu.
	ca. 479	Confucius dies.
	ca. 7-4	Jesus is born in Bethlehem in the Roman province of Judea.

Timeline *(continued)*

CE		
	ca. 7	At age twelve, Jesus accompanies his parents to the Passover feast in Jerusalem.
	ca. 26	Now about thirty, Jesus is baptized by his cousin, John the Baptist, and begins preaching in Judea and neighboring regions.
	ca. 28-30	John the Baptist is executed by King Herod; Jesus delivers the Sermon on the Mount.
	ca. 30-33	Jesus goes to Jerusalem, where he is arrested, tried, and crucified.
	ca. 570	Muhammad is born in Mecca, in Arabia.
	ca. 576	He is adopted by his uncle, Abu Talib.
	ca. 595	Muhammad marries a woman named Khadija.
	ca. 610	According to tradition, he receives his first revelation from the angel Gabriel.
	ca. 613	Muhammad preached in Mecca, where he is persecuted.
	ca. 622	He flees to the city of Yathrib, soon afterward renamed Medina.
	ca. 630	Most people in Mecca convert to Islam.
	ca. 632	Muhammad dies.

Sources

Introduction

p. 12,   "Most major religions . . ." H. W. F. Saggs, *Civilization Before Greece and Rome* (New Haven: Yale University Press, 1989), 267.

p. 12,   "The mainstream of Hinduism . . ." Ibid.

pp. 12-13, "Harappa, along with the other . . ." Tarini J. Carr, "The Harappan Civilization," Archaeology Online. http://www.archaeologyonline.net/artifacts/harappa-mohenjodaro.html

Chapter One: Krishna

p. 20,   "Mother, I didn't . . ." Edwin F. Bryant, trans., *Krishna: The Beautiful Legend of God* (New York: Penguin, 2003), 43.

p. 25,   "Just as you throw out . . ." Quoted in Steven Mitchell, ed., *Bhagavad Gita* (New York: Harmony, 2000) 49.

p. 26,   "I am the soul . . ." Ibid., 124, 130.

p. 27,   "I gladly accept . . ." Ibid., 304.

Chapter Two: Abraham

p. 32,   "I call Abraham . . ." Ken Spiro, "The World of Abraham," Judaism Online. http://www.simpletoremember.com/articles/a/abraham-bible/

p. 35,   "It is probable . . ." Cyrus H. Gordon, "Abraham and the Merchants of Ura," *Journal of Near Eastern Studies* 17 (1958): 30.

p. 36,   "Terah took Abraham . . ." Genesis 11:31.

p. 36,   "Go from your country . . ." Ibid., 12:1-2.

p. 39,   "When Abraham heard . . ." Ibid., 14:14-16.

p. 40,   "I will so greatly . . ." Ibid., 16:10.

pp. 41-42, "I will make my covenant . . ." Ibid., 17:2

p. 42,   "God needs a new kind of human . . ." Bruce Feiler, *Abraham: A Journey to the Heart of Three Faiths* (New York: William Morrow, 2002), 23.

pp. 42-43, "This is my covenant . . ." Genesis 17:10.

p. 43,   "You shall be circumcised . . ." Ibid., 17:11-14.

p. 43,   "Sarah, your wife . . ." Ibid., 17:19

p. 44,   "Abraham! . . ." Ibid., 22:1-2.

p. 45,   "Do not lay your hands . . ." Ibid., 22:12.

p. 46,   "a magnet of monotheism . . ." Feiler, *Abraham*, 4.

p. 49,   "After four thousand years . . ." Max Dimont, *Jews, God, and History* (New York: New American Library, 2004), 30.

Chapter Three: The Buddha

p. 54,   "In his [the elephant's] trunk . . ." Quoted in E. J. Thomas, *The Life of Buddha in Legend and History* (London: Kegan Paul, 2003), 31-32.

p. 56,   "Lily pools were made . . ." Quoted in Bhikkhu Nananoli, trans., *The Life of the Buddha According to the Pali Canon* (Seattle: Buddhist Publication Society, 2001), 8.

pp. 57-58, "bent as a roof gable . . ." Quoted in John M. Koller, *Oriental Philosophies* (New York: Scribner's, 1970), 106.

p. 58,   "I will [cut] off my hair . . ." Ibid., 108.

p. 59,   "Rough is the road . . ." Quoted in Clarence H. Hamilton, ed., *Buddhism: Selections from Buddhist Literature* (New York: Bobbs-Merrill, 1952) 18.

p. 60,   "My body reached a state . . ." Quoted in Nananoli, *The Life of the Buddha According to the Pali Canon*, 18.

pp. 60-61, "As soon as I ate . . ." Ibid., 21.

p. 61,   "Come what may . . ." Quoted in Eknath Easwaran, trans., *The Dhammapada* (Petaluma, CA: Niligri Press, 1990), 26.

p. 65,   "Be a lamp . . ." Ibid., 44.

p. 66,   "Work out your own salvation . . ." Quoted in "The Life of the Buddha," Vipassana Research Institute. http://www.vri.dhamma.org/publications/buddha1.html

Chapter Four: Confucius

p. 73, "My calculations . . ." Quoted in Jonathan Clements, *Confucius: A Biography* (UK: Sutton, 2004), 15.

p. 73, "The oxen and sheep . . ." Ibid.

pp. 73-74, "Do not do . . ." Quoted in Fung Yu-Lan, *A Short History of Chinese Philosophy*, Ed. Dirk Bodde (New York: Macmillan, 1948) 43.

p. 75, "Sincerity is the way . . ." Quoted in James Legge, trans., *The Teachings of Confucius* (El Paso: TX: Norte Press, 2005), 146.

p. 75, "By hearing the music . . ." Quoted in H. G. Creel, *Confucius and the Chinese Way* (New York: Harper & Row, 1960), 88.

p. 76, "I do not open up . . ." Quoted in Legge, *The Teachings of Confucius*, 34-35.

p. 76, "When you know a thing . . ." Ibid., 11.

p. 76, "When you see . . ." Quoted in Creel, *Confucius and the Chinese Way*, 92.

p. 79, "Mark this well . . ." Quoted in Clements, *Confucius: A Biography*, 30.

p. 79, "There is government . . ." Quoted in Legge, *The Teachings of Confucius*, 68.

p. 79, "To govern means . . ." Ibid., 69.

p. 85, "No intelligent monarch . . ." Quoted in E. W. F. Tomlin, *The Oriental Philosophers: An Introduction* (New York: Harper & Row, 1963), 264.

Chapter Five: Zoroaster

p. 94, "Speak to me . . ." Quoted in Mary P. Fisher, *Living Religions* (New York: Prentice Hall, 1991), 203.

p. 95, "I am Zoroaster . . ." Quoted in Loren H. Whitney, *Life and Teachings of Zoroaster the Great Persian* (Whitefish, MT: Kessinger Publishing, 2005), 62.

p. 98, "Even should my body be torn . . ." Ibid., 72.

pp. 98-99, "With the sacred mortar . . ." Quoted in A. V. Williams Jackson, *Zoroaster: the Prophet of Ancient Iran* (New York: Columbia University Press, 1919), 53.

p. 99,   "To what land . . ." Quoted in Mary P. Fisher, *Living Religions*, 204.

Chapter Six: Jesus

p. 110,   "The Messiah would come down . . ." A. N. Wilson, *Paul: The Mind of the Apostle* (New York: W. W. Norton, 2000), 7-8.

p. 115,   "Let it be so . . ." Matthew 3:15.

p. 118,   "Blessed are the poor . . ." Matthew 5:3-10.

p. 119,   "Take, eat . . ." Matthew 26:26-28.

p. 121,   "You are the Christ . . ." Matthew 16:16.

p. 122,   "It is written . . ." Luke 24:46-49.

p. 123,   "About noon . . ." Acts: 22:6-10.

Chapter Seven: Muhammad

p. 134,   "I am not [one] . . ." Quoted in Tariq Ramadan, *In the Footsteps of the Prophet: Lessons from the Life of Muhammad* (New York: Oxford University Press, 2007), 29.

p. 135,   "Recite in the name of . . ." Quoted in Karen Armstrong, *Muhammad: A Biography of the Prophet* (San Francisco, CA: HarperSanFrancisco, 1993), 83.

p. 136,   "When I was midway . . ." Ibid.

pp. 138-139, "The message was similar . . ." Erica Fraser, "Muhammad." http://www.ucalgary.ca/applied_history/tutor/islam/beginnings/

p. 139,   "I am but . . ." Quoted in Ramadan, *In the Footsteps of the Prophet*, 46.

pp. 143-144, "In 624, Muhammad decided . . ." Fraser, "Muhammad."

p. 145,   "O People, listen . . ." Quoted in Yahiya Emerick, *Muhammad* (Indianapolis, IN: Alpha Penguin, 2002), 286.

p. 145,   "My Lord, help me . . ." Ibid., 292.

p. 145,   "There is no god . . ." Quoted in Erica Fraser, "Islamic Beliefs and Practices," http://www.ucalgary.ca/applied_history/tutor/islam/beginnings/.

Bibliography

Abd-Ru-Shin. *Zoroaster: Life and Work of the Forerunner in Persia.* Mt. Vernon, Ohio: Grail Foundation Press, 1996.

Armstrong, Karen. *Buddha.* New York: Viking Penguin, 2001.

———. *Islam: A Short History.* New York: Modern Library, 2000.

———. *Muhammad: A Biography of the Prophet.* San Francisco: HarperSan Francisco, 1993.

Aslan, Reza. *No God but God: The Origins, Evolution, and Future of Islam.* New York: Random House, 2005.

Bodhi, Bhikkhu, ed. *In the Buddha's Words: An Anthology of Discourses From the Pali Canon.* Boston: Wisdom, 2005.

Borg, Marcus. *Jesus: Uncovering the Life, Teachings, and Relevance of a Religious Revolutionary.* New York: HarperOne, 2008.

Boyce, Mary. *Zoroastrians: Their Religious Beliefs and Practices.* London: Routledge and Kegan Paul, 1985.

Bryant, Edwin, trans. *Krishna: The Beautiful Legends of God.* New York: Penguin Putnam, 2003.

Choksy, Jamsheed K. *Purity and Pollution in Zoroastrianism: Triumph over Evil.* Austin: University of Texas Press, 1989.

Clements, Jonathan. *Confucius: A Biography.* Charleston, SC: History Press, 2008.

Dimmitt, Cornelia, and van Buitenen. *Classical Hindu Mythology: A Reader in The Sanskrit Puranas.* Philadelphia: Temple University Press, 1978.

Easwaran, Eknath, trans. *The Dhammapada.* Petaluma, CA: Niligri Press, 1990.

Emerick, Yahiya. *Muhammad*, Indianapolis: Alpha Penguin, 2002.

Gonzalez, Justo L. *A Concise History of Christian Doctrine.* Nashville: Abingdon, 2006.

———. *The Story of Christianity, Volume I, The Early Church to the Dawn of the Reformation.* New York: HarperOne, 2010.

Grant, Michael. *Jesus: An Historian's Review of the Gospels.* New York: Scribner's, 1995.

Giullaume, Alfred. *Islam.* New York: Penguin, 1982.

Insler, Stanley. *The Gathas of Zarathustra.* Leiden: E. J. Brill, 1975.

Jackson, A. V. Williams. *Zoroaster: The Prophet of Ancient Iran.* New York: Columbia University Press, 2005.

Jaspers, Karl. *Socrates, Buddha, Confucius, Jesus.* New York: Harcourt, Brace & World, 1985.

Koller, John M. *Asian Philosophies.* Englewood Cliffs, NJ: Prentice-Hall: 2002.

Legge, James, trans. *The Teachings of Confucius: The Analects, The Great Learning, The Doctrine of the Mean.* El Paso: Norte Press, 2005.

Lewis, Bernard. *Islam in History.* Chicago: Open Court, 2001.

McManners, John, ed. *The Oxford History of Christianity.* Oxford: Oxford University Press, 2002.

Menon, Ramesh. *Blue God: A Life of Krishna.* Lincoln, NE: Writers Club Press, 2000.

Mitchell, Steven. *Bhagavad Gita.* New York: Harmony, 2000.

Molloy, Michael. *Experiencing the World Religions.* CA: Mayfield, 1999.

Nelson, Walter. *Buddha: His Life and His Teaching.* New York: Putnam, 2000.

Nylan, Michael. *Lives of Confucius.* New York: Doubleday Religion, 2010.

Renan, Ernest. *The Life of Jesus.* San Diego: Book Tree Publishing, 2007.

Sanders, E. P. *The Historical Figure of Jesus.* New York: Penguin, 1996.

Smith, Huston. *The World's Religions.* New York: HarperCollins, 1991.

Thomas, E. J. *The Life of Buddha in Legend and History.* London: Kegan Paul, 2003.

Wilson, A. N. *Paul: The Mind of the Apostle.* New York: W. W. Norton, 2000.

Web sites

Assorted Tales of Krishna
http://www.thaiexotictreasures.com/krishna.
html#Summary%20of%20the%20story%20of%20Krishna

Buddhism
http://www.bbc.co.uk/religion/religions/buddhism/

Children's Stories About Krishna
www.surrealist.org/gurukula/storymatters/krishna.html

From Jesus to Christ: The First Christians
http://www.pbs.org/wgbh/pages/frontline/shows/religion/

The Gospels and Jesus
http://www.wsu.edu/~dee/CHRIST/CHRIST.HTM

Life and Teachings of Buddha
http://www.buddhanet.net

Life of Muhammad
http://www.pbs.org/muhammad/timeline_html.shtml

Paintings Showing Scenes from Buddha's Life
http://www.asianart.com/exhibitions/svision/i27.html

Paul of Tarsus
http://www.wsu.edu/~dee/CHRIST/CHRIST.HTM

The Prophet Muhammad
http://www.pbs.org/muhammad/muhammadand.shtml

Sayings of Confucius
http://www.age-of-the-sage.org/historical/biography/confucius.html

Zoroaster, the Persian Prophet
http://www.crystalinks.com/z.html

Index

Photo Credits

10-11: Used under license from iStockphoto.com

14-15: Used under license from iStockphoto.com

16-17: Used under license from iStockphoto.com

18-19: Used under license from iStockphoto.com

34: Courtesy of Crates/Chaim the Bipolar

46-47: Peter Willi/Getty Images

50-51: Used under license from iStockphoto.com

53: Used under license from iStockphoto.com

56: Used under license from iStockphoto.com

59: Used under license from iStockphoto.com

60-61: Edgloris Marys / Alamy

67: World Religions Photo Library / Alamy

68-69: World History Archive / Alamy

70-71: Used under license from iStockphoto.com

75: Lou-Foto / Alamy

85: Used under license from iStockphoto.com

86-87: Felipe Trueba / Alamy

92: The Art Archive / Alamy

96: The Art Archive / Alamy

101: The Art Archive / Alamy

105: The Art Archive / Alamy

106-107: Archive Images / Alamy

108: Used under license from iStockphoto.com

112-113: Archive Images / Alamy

116: Archive Images / Alamy

125: The Art Archive / Alamy

129: Used under license from iStockphoto.com

132: Courtesy of Bluemangoa2z

Book cover and interior design by Derrick Carroll Creative.